LE JOUR SE LÈVE

CINÉ-FILES: The French Film Guides
Series Editor: Ginette Vincendeau

From the pioneering days of the Lumière brothers' Cinématographe in 1895, France has been home to perhaps the most consistently vibrant film culture in the world, producing world-class directors and stars, and a stream of remarkable movies, from popular genre films to cult avant-garde works. Many of these have found a devoted audience outside France, and the arrival of DVD is now enabling a whole new generation to have access to contemporary titles as well as the great classics of the past.

The Ciné-Files French Film Guides build on this welcome new access, offering authoritative and entertaining guides to some of the most significant titles, from the silent era to the early twenty-first century. Written by experts in French cinema, the books combine extensive research with the author's distinctive, sometimes provocative perspective on each film. The series will thus build up an essential collection on great French classics, enabling students, teachers and lovers of French cinema both to learn more about their favourite films and make new discoveries in one of the world's richest bodies of cinematic work.

Published and forthcoming Ciné-Files include:

À bout de souffle (Jean-Luc Godard, 1960) – Ramona Fotiade
Alphaville (Jean-Luc Godard, 1965) – Chris Darke
Amélie (Jean-Pierre Jeunet, 2001) – Isabelle Vanderschelden
Casque d'or (Jacques Becker, 1952) – Sarah Leahy
Un chien andalou (Luis Buñuel, 1929) – Elza Adamowicz
Cléo de 5 à 7 (Agnès Varda, 1961) – Valerie Orpen
Le Corbeau (Henri-Georges Clouzot, 1943) – Judith Mayne
Les Diaboliques (Henri-Georges Clouzot, 1955) – Susan Hayward
La Grande Illusion (Jean Renoir, 1937) – Martin O'Shaughnessy
La Haine (Mathieu Kassovitz, 1995) – Ginette Vincendeau
Le Jour se lève (Marcel Carné, 1939) – Ben McCann
La Règle du jeu (Jean Renoir, 1939) – Keith Reader
La Reine Margot (Patrice Chéreau, 1994) – Julianne Pidduck
Rififi (Jules Dassin, 1955) – Alastair Phillips

French Film Guide

LE JOUR SE LÈVE

Ben McCann

I.B. TAURIS
LONDON · NEW YORK

**Arts & Humanities
Research Council**

This publication is supported by the AHRC.

Each year the AHRC provides funding from the Government to support research and postgraduate study in the arts and humanities. Only applications of the highest quality are funded and the range of research supported by this investment of public funds not only provides social and cultural benefits but also contributes to the economic success of the UK. For further information on the AHRC, please go to: www.ahrc.ac.uk

Published in 2014 by I.B.Tauris & Co. Ltd
6 Salem Road, London W2 4BU
175 Fifth Avenue, New York NY 10010
www.ibtauris.com

Distributed in the United States and Canada Exclusively by Palgrave Macmillan
175 Fifth Avenue, New York NY 10010

ISBN: 978 1 78076 592 1
eISBN: 978 0 85773 474 7

A full CIP record for this book is available from the British Library
A full CIP record is available from the Library of Congress

Library of Congress Catalog Card Number: available

Typesetting and eBook by Tetragon, London
Printed and bound by CPI Group (UK) Ltd, Croydon, CR0 4YY

... I walked into the cinema. The film had already started. It was a good film and I gave it my undivided attention. When it was over I walked out and looked up at the marquee. 'Le Jour se lève' was the title. 'Amen to that,' I said.

The Dud Avocado, Elaine Dundy

For my parents, Geoff and Eirlys

Contents

Acknowledgements

This book began life many years ago, over lunch at the Au Petit Fer à Cheval in Paris, when Sue Harris suggested I write about *Le Jour se lève*. My thanks, then, to Sue. I'd particularly like to thank Ginette Vincendeau for offering me the chance to contribute to this marvellous series, and for her immense patience, feedback and guidance along the way. There were times when this book looked unlikely ever to see the light of day, and so I offer my sincere gratitude to both Ginette, and Philippa Brewster at I.B.Tauris, for their intuition and editorial expertise. My appreciation also to Geoff Schilling for assistance with the images, and Pat Fitzgerald for her copy-editing work.

I'm also most grateful to the staff at the British Film Institute National Library and the Bibliothèque du Film (BiFi) in Paris, and to the Faculty of Humanities and Social Sciences at the University of Adelaide for their financial support and assistance.

Finally, a very special thanks to Jacqueline, who kept me on track, and to Monty, who was born as the last chapter was being written.

Synopsis

France. An unnamed industrial suburb, the present day. The film unfolds in a series of flashbacks.

A worker in a sandblasting factory, François (Jean Gabin), kills unscrupulous dog-trainer Valentin (Jules Berry) and barricades himself into his room on the top floor of an apartment block. He is soon besieged by the police, who fail in an attempt to shoot themselves into the room. François pushes a large wardrobe against the door, sealing himself in. He begins smoking, pacing around the apartment, and reminiscing.

In a series of three flashbacks, punctuated by sequences in the present, it is revealed that François is romantically involved with a young florist, Françoise (Jacqueline Laurent), and with Clara (Arletty), Valentin's assistant at a nearby *café-concert* show. Valentin grows jealous of François, as the older man was once casually involved with Françoise. After spying on François and Clara, Valentin falsely claims to be Françoise's father, even though both François and Françoise are revealed to be orphans (and share a name day). Valentin does not want François to continue his courtship of Françoise. François and Françoise meet in a greenhouse, and she promises to not see Valentin again. They tenderly confess their love for each other for the first time. Valentin eventually confronts François in his room with a revolver. An extended argument ensues (during which François threatens to throw Valentin out of the apartment window), and provoked, François shoots and kills Valentin.

François becomes hysterical and screams to his friends and co-workers who have gathered in the small square beneath the apartment block. As day breaks, a delirious Françoise is tended to by Clara. Riot police arrive and disperse the crowd. Two policemen climb over the roof of François's apartment and throw a tear-gas canister into his room. At that same moment, François, overcome with despair and grief, shoots himself through the heart. The film ends with the sound of a ringing alarm clock and tear-gas clouds filling the room around François's body.

Introduction

I saw it seventeen times in one month [...] and four times in one day, each
time leaving the cinema dazzled and engulfed by an inexplicable sense of pain
and pleasure. (Claude Sautet)[1]

I have written of this film in superlatives before. I have seen it four times and
still it seems to have no flaws. It's absolutely national and absolutely universal.
(Richard Winnington)[2]

To begin with, an aside. Nineteen thirty-nine is often held up as Hollywood's
annus mirabilis. A quick glance at some of its marquee releases – *The Wizard
of Oz, Stagecoach, Ninotchka, Mr Smith Goes to Washington, The Grapes of
Wrath* – sums up what André Bazin termed the 'genius of the system'. The
entire corpus of classical Hollywood cinema might be cloned from these
films, but time and again it is *Gone with the Wind* that critics, historians
and viewers hold up as the exemplary film product from 1939, and it is
still that film that achieves the most cultural purchase today. Similarly, in
France, where this book is set, a whole wonderful range of films was released
in 1939 that have, for one reason or another, always been obliged to make
way for its most canonical masterpiece, *La Règle du jeu*.[3] It is this film that
casts a shadow over history books, Top Ten lists and university film courses
to this day, whereas contemporaneous releases as diverse as *Circonstances
atténuantes, Ils étaient neuf célibataires, Le Dernier Tournant* and *Menaces*
are airbrushed out of official cultural discourse, despite encapsulating very
exact expressions of 1930s French film culture and practice. Add to that
list Marcel Carné's *Le Jour se lève*, released three weeks before *La Règle du
jeu*. Those expressions – political, social, emotional, aesthetic – coalesce
to a remarkable degree. A film of dead ends and despair, we remain today
beguiled by its melancholic romanticism and eloquent fatalism.

For many, *Le Jour se lève* is not Marcel Carné's best film. That honour
usually goes to *Les Enfants du paradis* (1945), the film that François Truffaut
once admitted he would trade in his entire back catalogue to have made.[4] But
for me, it is its bittersweet, pared-down narrative, its economy of gesture and
its expressive decor that makes *Le Jour se lève* Carné's masterpiece. Working

at the interface of popular and auteur aesthetics, Carné represented the very best of the French studio system by the time pre-production began on the film in late 1938. Shuttling between different registers, tones and textures, he was immensely collaborative, capable of marshalling the resources of the studio, adept at pictorial composition, and was a steady overseer of populist and accessible films that struck a resonant chord with audiences.

Pick up any history of French cinema and *Le Jour se lève*'s iconic images stare back at us: François gazing forlornly out of a window, Valentin cajoling his dogs, Arletty playfully covering her body as she steps out of a shower. By 1939, Carné had become the leading standard bearer of the French Poetic Realist aesthetic. A film style that combined romantic-fatalist narratives with claustrophobic milieus and an accentuated *mise-en-scène*, Poetic Realism was epitomized by directors like Carné, Pierre Chenal and Julien Duvivier. Taken as a whole, these works were strong precursors to American *film noir*, and it was Carné's own contributions that were the most impressive. *Le Jour se lève* is clearly influenced by the austere visual style of German Expressionists like F.W. Murnau and Fritz Lang, while its recurring urban iconography and character types recalled Carné's early mentors René Clair and Jacques Feyder.

Le Jour se lève is a clairvoyant film that neatly synthesizes the filaments and fears of its historical moment. More than any other released in Europe in the late 1930s, it peered into a near future pregnant with foreboding and pessimism. Carné spent his whole life resisting barometrical readings of his films, but it is hard to avoid reading *Le Jour se lève* as shorthand for the state of the French nation in 1939, a place full of sombre corners and encroaching extinction. It is very much a 'mood film', and a confirmation of national self-doubt and existential despair. Despite the ironic implications of its title – *Daybreak* – the film is engorged with a melancholy that corresponds to a whole raft of political and social contexts: the *dégringolade* (collapse) of the Popular Front, the aftermath of the Munich Agreement and the perceived betrayal of the working class. Less than 12 months after the film was released, France capitulated to the German army, and a whole new 'daybreak' would emerge across France until the summer of 1944.

Structurally too, *Le Jour se lève* is daring and highly influential. It is one of the first films to employ a complex narrative syntax, full of the flashbacks, ellipses and object symbolism that pre-dated the American *film noir* template of doomed, decent men jammed into a claustrophobic architecture by nearly ten years. It was a film that influenced Orson Welles, John Huston and Howard Hawks, but also young French directors like Jean-Pierre Melville, Jules Dassin and Jacques Becker, who borrowed Carné's interleaving of the visual and the psychological to create similar narratives of despair and gloom. Think of the final shot of Belmondo's empty hat in Melville's *Le Doulos* (1962) – a symbol, like the ringing clock at the end of the *Le Jour se lève*, for the death of a good man. Or Serge Reggiani in Becker's *Casque d'or* (1952), guillotined in the street for having killed a man who had corrupted the woman he loves. As a performance piece, the film would mark the high point of the careers of its lead actors. Jules Berry was never more oleaginous as Valentin, the original showman *raté*; Jacqueline Laurent's china-doll fragility was rarely captured so expertly again, and Arletty, so luminous for Carné in *Les Enfants du paradis* and so guttural in *Hôtel du Nord*, nearly steals the show. Jacques Prévert never wrote more lyrical dialogue, Alexandre Trauner never designed sets more expressive. And Carné, ruthlessly punned by Bazin as 'disincarnated' after the war, was rarely again able to marshal the talents of his technical team in such a controlled and sustained way. French Poetic Realism, a style and a sensibility that Carné did much to develop and export, despite his protestations, reached its apotheosis in 1939, and with *Le Jour se lève*, the legacy of the Golden Age of French Cinema was clinched. And of course, *Le Jour se lève* remains above all a film for, with and about Jean Gabin. Perhaps French cinema's greatest actor, he dominates the film, appearing in nigh on every scene, alternately explosive and tender, nonchalant and nostalgic. Whether he is drinking milk from a bottle or reading shipping reports, there is a wholesale identification with François that, as Dudley Andrew reminds us, is similar to those 1930s cinema-goers who watched Gabin's films 'putting all obstructions from their minds, and virtually climbing through the screen to join the figure of Gabin as he groped through his poetic realist films'.[5] Nowhere was this pact played out more dolefully than in *Le Jour se lève*, where Bolop the teddy bear's 'one sad eye and one cheerful eye' stand not just for François but for a whole swathe of French society marooned between opposing force fields of the Popular Front and France's post-Munich malaise.

Chapter 1 of this book will trace the context of the film's genesis and examine the socio-historical backdrop and state of French cinema on the eve of the war. Reviews and studies of *Le Jour se lève* all tend to constellate around five aspects: structure, set design, style, politics and performance. Accordingly, Chapter 2 will provide an in-depth analysis of the structural and stylistic aspects of the film, while Chapter 3 will concentrate on political and performance strands. Both chapters contain sequence analyses of four key scenes in the film. Finally, Chapter 4 will explore the reception of the film in France during a time of great national upheaval, and will also compare *Le Jour se lève* to its 1947 American remake, *The Long Night*.

Notes

1   Claude Sautet, 'Le Jour se lève', Positif, June 1994, p. 126.

2   Richard Winnington, 'A slight case of murder' (11 May 1946), repr. in Drawn and Quartered (London: Saturn, 1948), p. 54.

3   Richard Roud has written of La Règle du jeu that 'if France were destroyed tomorrow and nothing remained but this film, the whole country and its civilization could be reconstructed from it' (Richard Roud, 'Jean Renoir: to 1939', Cinema: A Critical Dictionary (London: Secker and Warburg, 1980), vol. 2, p. 841).

4   Carné recalls the compliment in his autobiography La Vie à belles dents (Paris: Pierre Belfond, 1989), p. 355.

5   Dudley Andrew, Mists of Regret: Culture and Sensibility in Classic French Film (Princeton: Princeton University Press, 1995), p. 325.

1   Context and Planning

[T]he most Carnésian of Carné's films[1]

Le Jour se lève was fashioned out of an alliance between four of the decade's most important artistic personalities – director Marcel Carné, screenwriter Jacques Prévert, designer Alexandre Trauner and actor Jean Gabin. The four had already worked together in one combination or another on Carné's four previous 1930s films and, *sans* Gabin, they would reunite under extraordinary pressure and privation during the Occupation to film *Les Enfants du paradis*. Yet it was on *Le Jour se lève*, that 'masterpiece of European poetic realism',[2] that the team crystallized most perfectly the intersection between design and performance, planning and execution, and cooperation and collaboration. Working together, each positioned himself firmly at the heart of the film's evolutionary process. Comments and ideas would move backwards and forwards regarding script issues, camera position, design strategies and choice of actors. Nothing was fixed or immutable. British filmmaker and historian Paul Rotha once noted how '[n]early every film of interest which has originated from France has been the product of an individualistic artistic mind',[3] an implicit acknowledgement that a director's personal imprimatur inflected many of the key films of the 1930s. Yet this conviction that Carné is the sole auteur behind *Le Jour se lève* runs the risk of espousing a romantic view of the film as the product of a solitary inspiration. Instead, Carné should be conceptualized as an orchestrator of a multitude of different talents, a conductor or 'master of a grand style reminiscent of D.W. Griffith at his most flamboyant'.[4] Rather than privileging the director as the sole creative presence, it is more appropriate to see Carné as the follower of a Hollywood-style model of production, running counter to traditional auteurist approaches to

French cinema. If Carné's creativity was 'best energised through interaction with the imaginative strengths of his finest co-workers',[5] it was because he surrounded himself with other perfectionists whose fastidiousness paved the way for the development of the Poetic Realist aesthetic. This climate of collaborative filmmaking is essentially symbiotic, with each member of the team acting and reacting to each other's ideas; what Jean-Pierre Jeancolas has termed a reproduction of 'reality by consensus'.[6] It reveals an inherently utopian mode of production practice flourishing in France at the time – artists who worked closely with one another, who critiqued, commented upon and refined each other's creative output. This climate of reciprocal filmmaking opened up the possibility of collaborative innovation and project-specific achievement in ways that were unprecedented'.[7] Moreover, the success of *Le Jour se lève* is symptomatic of 1930s French cinema's transnational flexibility and its dynamic circulation of diverse cultural influences, whereby an Eastern European set designer and a German cinematographer could successfully cross-pollinate within a French context to inaugurate a new range of textural properties. To understand the formal beauty of *Le Jour se lève*, then, it is necessary to reframe the film as the product of many different imaginations coalescing in a quite remarkable way at a specific time of transition in the French film industry. *Le Jour se lève* remains as much a socio-historical phenomenon as an industrio-aesthetic one, and it is at these points of convergence between industry, context and personnel that our exploration of the film begins.

Carné and the team

When examining Carné's career, the same questions always arise. Were his films collaborations in which collective input was privileged over the product of a solitary inspiration? Were the films successful because of or in spite of Carné? Is Carné an auteur, or merely a fine orchestrator? He certainly surrounded himself with the best technicians and personnel of the 1930s, each of whom brought individual talents to the filmmaking process. *Le Jour se lève* is ultimately the apotheosis of a number of artists and craftsmen, many of whom never reached such pinnacles of achievement again. Rather than referring to late-1930s French cinema as 'an affair of individuals',[8] it is instead necessary to talk of mutuality, of partnership and of cross-cultural vibrancy. When it came to assembling his team, Carné did not have to look far.

Marcel Carné (director)

Born in Paris in 1906, Marcel Carné epitomizes the structural flexibility in the French film industry in the 1930s. Although this 'tidy pessimist and adroit technician'[9] continued making films well into the 1970s, it will be for his output between 1936 and 1946 that Carné will be forever enshrined in cinema histories. He became one of the most successful directors of the period and the epitome of the Golden Age tradition of filmmaking. Despite the critical neglect into which he fell in the years immediately after the Liberation, he remains one of the decade's *monstres sacrés* and an enduring presence in classical French cinema.

Dubbed a 'megalomaniac of decor' by André Bazin,[10] Carné's concept of filmmaking indicates a style reliant upon constructed urban landscapes and meticulous pictorial composition. This perceived lack of spontaneity tends to see Carné relegated to the lower tier of the 1930s pantheon behind the likes of Renoir and Vigo. Whereas they searched for a cinema predicated upon impulsiveness and immediacy, Carné was criticized for favouring a cinema that was rigorously pre-planned, airless, bereft of life and frigid.[11] Such criticisms have been part of the discourse surrounding Carné since the release of *Les Portes de la nuit* in 1946, damaging his pre-war reputation and effectively undermining the achievement of *Le Jour se lève*.

After rejecting his father's trade of cabinetmaking, Carné originally trained as a photographer and became interested in filmmaking while working as a journalist at *Cinémagazine* at the end of the 1920s. The transition to filmmaking was as instinctive as it was improvisatory. After a chance meeting with director Jacques Feyder's wife, Françoise Rosay, at a dinner party, Feyder hired Carné as camera assistant on *Les Nouveaux Messieurs* (1928). Despite being given little of consequence to do, the experience was a valuable one, not least because it allowed Carné to watch and learn.[12]

In between unhappy spells as assistant to Richard Oswald on *Cagliostro* (1929), and as assistant director to René Clair on *Sous les toits de Paris* a year later, Carné's first work proper was the semi-Impressionist *Nogent, eldorado du dimanche* (1929). Conceived on a whim – 'I bought a camera and some film and I made the film […] I did it to see if I could do something'[13] – *Nogent* was a silent documentary that showed the simple pleasures of the Parisian working class on a Sunday afternoon excursion along the River Marne. Critics were impressed by Carné's sincerity towards his subject matter and his grasp of pictorialism. Such sensitivity to populist iconography and topography became key motifs of Carné's oeuvre and recalls the community narratives that typified the Impressionist painters like Sisley and Renoir, whom Carné admired. The ultimate theme of the film is escape and freedom; a self-willed Edenic sojourn from the travails of Paris, and as such introduces the defining motif of Carné's films – characters 'seek[ing] ceaselessly to break from the claustrophobia of their physical and spiritual environment and return to an earthly paradise'.[14]

After Feyder returned from a stint in Hollywood, Carné reunited with his mentor and assisted him on *Le Grand Jeu* (1933), *Pension Mimosas* (1934) and *La Kermesse héroïque* (1935). Carné's first solo film was the moody melodrama *Jenny*. This story about doomed love and star-crossed lovers marked the beginnings of a romantic fatalist mode of address that would endure up to *Les Portes de la nuit*. Françoise Rosay stars as Jenny, who manages a sleazy Paris nightclub owned by Benoît (Charles Vanel). Matters are complicated when Jenny's daughter (Lisette Lanvin) becomes romantically involved with racing-car driver Lucien (Albert Préjean), whom Jenny passionately loves. When Benoît and his hunchbacked assistant (Jean-Louis Barrault) take revenge on Lucien, putting him in hospital, Jenny borrows money to pay for his hospital fees. Despite her actions, mother loses both daughter and lover at the end, and is destined to remain at Club Jenny.

Jenny was an important step for Carné, for although it took more films for the Poetic Realist aesthetic to be articulated, it was partially delineated here. On a collaborative level, *Jenny* also established the creative partnerships Carné would return to for the next decade. Jacques Prévert was an integral part of the team, while the casting of major star Rosay reveals the typical Carné product: star-studded and technically proficient. Stylistically, the mixture of 'theatrical' melodrama and Poetic Realist styles throughout the film is striking. A character remarks at one point that 'Life is funny […] It always has people entering and exiting; arrivals and departures, departures and arrivals'. This comment not only reinforces the insistent sense of fate, destiny and life-as-theatre in Carné's work, but also verbalizes the tension in *Jenny* between the theatrical and the poetic. Carné juxtaposes theatrical interior scenes (the nightclub, the café, the hospital) with exterior Poetic Realist motifs such as the canal side and the railway bridge. These motifs of industrial iconography – pylons, cranes, railway tracks, bridges – suggest Carné's emergent pictorial style and anticipate the grimy *loci classici* of his later works. The film feels experimental in both mode of address and style; an amplification of themes and ideas distilled from his close observations of Clair and Feyder. There is greater camera mobility than one tends to find in later Carné films, and recourse to pictorial importing and documentary footage to heighten the reality effect. All of this reinforces the idea that *Jenny* is incrementally sketching out a new aesthetic, underpinning the optimism of the mid-1930s with a stylized despondency. If French cinema 'passed into adulthood'[15] in this period, then *Jenny* is the harbinger of that maturation. If Carné's next film, *Drôle de drame* (1937), remains an oddity in an increasingly homogenous corpus of films, the film continues the progression of the Carné aesthetic. Irwin Molyneux (Michel Simon) plays a botanist who loves nothing more than his mimosas, but, under orders from his wife (Rosay, again), also moonlights as a crime novelist under the pen name Felix Chapel. After a man known as the Butcher Killer blames Chapel for his own crimes, the Bishop of Bedford (Louis Jouvet) launches a crusade against Chapel's 'dangerous' novels, and thus ensues a steadily frenetic interplay of sexual sublimation and mistaken identity. Like *Jenny*, it develops Carné's working practices and assembles more members of the team (this time, designer Alexandre Trauner and composer Maurice Jaubert) that would go on to make *Le Jour se lève*. The film, set in Victorian London, remains a cult classic among Carné enthusiasts – those who berate the director for lacking a sense of humour might do well to recall scenes of Louis Jouvet in a kilt, or Jean-Louis Barrault killing butchers out of his fondness for sheep – and against this backdrop of broad farce emerges an anti-clerical satire targeted at the Church and the Establishment. Turk suggests that the film's moral is clear: 'the survival of the bourgeoisie is dependent upon the unrewarded labours of the proletariat';[16] sentiments that anticipate the darker class struggles at the heart of *Le Jour se lève*. With its explorations of the tensions between reality and appearance, its creation of a meticulously rendered atmosphere (such as the Limehouse back alleys and Molyneux's greenhouse) and its expressive camera movements, *Drôle de drame* remains very much a part of the Carné corpus. The film (released as *Bizarre, Bizarre* in Britain and America) is Carné's most playful film, full of ludic wordplay, visual playfulness and intentionally melodramatic performances.

The release of *Le Quai des brumes* and *Hôtel du Nord* in 1938 brought Carné critical and commercial acclaim. While both films continued the themes of Carné's previous works, they also crystallized his textural style, imbuing the doom-laden narratives with moody long shots of disaffected lovers and army deserters offset by witty and nostalgic *bons mots*. *Le Quai des brumes* is an adaptation of Pierre Mac Orlan's short story, and stars Jean Gabin as Jean, a deserting soldier who hitches a ride into Le Havre and ends up in a lonely bar on the outskirts of town. He falls in love with Nelly (Michèle Morgan), falls foul of her lascivious guardian (Michel Simon) and is eventually killed by local gangster (Pierre Brasseur). Carné and Prévert transposed the action from Paris's Montmartre district to the port town of Le Havre. The change works well – the sense of urban isolation and claustrophobia juxtaposed to the wide expanse of the sea is a vivid metaphor for the fatalism inherent in the story. Carné's directorial flourishes also hinted at a development in object symbolism that coheres more fully in *Le Jour se lève* – the ship in a bottle and Nelly's translucent raincoat are paraphrases of the themes of stasis and ephemerality running throughout the narrative. Thiher suggests that several of Carné's themes recur in the film, most notably 'the impossibility of love in a world given over to inexorable hostility'.[17] These notions, along with the gratuitousness of evil, would reappear in *Le Jour se lève*. *Le Quai des brumes* features two sordid characters, each diametrically opposed to Jean. Nelly's guardian Zabel is brutally killed by Jean in what can be seen as a conventional working-out of Oedipal tensions, while Jean is himself gunned down at the end of the film by the jealous Lucien. Both Zabel and Lucien are prototypes of Valentin in *Le Jour se lève*. All three, crucially, are bourgeois, and all are alternately domineering and dismissive, manipulative and untrustworthy. *Le Quai des brumes* remains Carné's most coldly formal work, bespeaking a more transgressive content to Carné's oeuvre than simply pretty sets and star actors. The film's skewed approach to sexual politics mirrors the relationship issues in *Le Jour se lève*: Nelly is configured at the outset as Lucien's 'girl', but when that ownership is undermined by Jean, the end result can only be emasculation for either Lucien or Jean. This triangulation of desire coupled with the funfair bumper-car scene ('a metaphoric rendering of France's chaotic politics'[18]) anticipates the socio-historical contextualization of *Le Jour se lève* and Carné's emerging fascination with masculinity, crime and power hierarchies.

The only film not written by Prévert in this period, *Hôtel du Nord* was a further consolidation of the Carné team.[19] Adapted from Eugène Dabit's prize-winning novel, the deceptively simple story charts the comings and goings at the eponymous hotel on the banks of the Canal St Martin in Paris. Characters include the young couple Pierre (Jean-Pierre Aumont) and Renée (Annabella), who arrive at the hotel but fail to carry out their planned suicide pact, and the story features the turbulent relationship between prostitute Raymonde (Arletty) and her reformed gangster lover Edmond (Louis Jouvet). *Hôtel du Nord* may have lacked Prévert's acerbic edge, but Henri Jeanson's script was both cynical and melancholic about the possibility of love, and included Arletty's famous 'Atmosphère, atmosphère' scene. It is also a masterpiece of production design and performance. The verisimilitude of

Trauner's sets anticipated the architectural expressivity he would bring to *Le Jour se lève*, and Arletty's role as the 'tart with the heart' would be modified and modulated in her later role as Clara. The film resonates with themes of imprisonment, disillusionment and the impossibility of escape, providing parallels with *Le Quai des brumes* and *Le Jour se lève*.

What *Drôle de drame*, *Le Quai des brumes* and *Hôtel du Nord* most notably clarified was Carné's total reliance upon built sets. These enclosed studio environments were necessities, given the stories he wanted to tell. The narrative and visual styles relied upon cramped spatial configurations in keeping with the romantic-fatalist aspect of his narratives. The use of intimate settings and symbolic objects is a trend that can be traced back to the German *Kammerspielfilm* tradition.[20] F.W. Murnau's films exemplified this style, most notably *Der letzte Mann/The Last Laugh* (1924), which anticipates the architectural and visual motifs in Carné's darker films. Murnau's bleak settings and slow camera movements were distinct formal correlates to his studies of psychological breakdown (what Carné himself described as a 'langage plastique'[21]). *Le Jour se lève* is characterized by a similar claustrophobic dramaturgy and a visual style that provided exact correspondences with individual emotion. Carné had already written extensively about Murnau's films in *Cinémagazine* in the early 1930s, and his debt to the director and the wider traditions of German Expressionism is clearly distilled in his 1930s films.[22] It is probably no more than coincidence that *Le Jour se lève* (*Daybreak*) shares its title with Murnau's most technically accomplished film, *Sunrise*. This film, often regarded as the greatest of all silent films, was released in 1927 when Carné's love for chiaroscuro textures, expansive sets and doomed romantic protagonists was still in its inception. Nevertheless, it is clear that the heritage of German Expressionism, and Murnau in particular, runs through Carné's work in several intersecting ways.

Jacques Prévert (screenwriter)

Few writers enjoyed as fruitful a creative partnership with a director as Jacques Prévert did with Marcel Carné. Over a period of eight films from 1936 to 1950, the two worked symbiotically together, sensitive to each other's creative instincts and both understanding the kind of narrative that was required for each individual film.[23] The importance of Prévert to Carné's most accomplished films has led many to question the extent of the director's authorship. For Truffaut, Carné merely 'renders in images films created by Jacques Prévert';[24] for others, the decline of Carné after 1950s can be largely attributed to his break with Prévert. Such debates are valid, but draw attention away from the conceptual richness of Carné's 1930s and 1940s work. Prévert's most impressive achievement in *Le Quai des brumes* and *Le Jour se lève* was to eke out of Carné's necessarily pessimistic worldview a poetry and an optimism that both underpinned and undermined the austerity of the image. Because the coming of sound had 'led to a new interest in forms of what can be broadly termed "realism"',[25] screenwriters in the early 1930s became increasingly crucial to the development of a distinctive style of French cinema. *Dialoguistes* like Henri Jeanson, Charles Spaak and Prévert came to the fore because they were skilled at embracing sound's potential for democratizing subject matter and bringing the concerns of the working class into a popular medium. Variations of dialect, accent and idiom made their way into screenplays, as scripts sought to represent the socio-political diversity enshrined in the accession of the Popular Front governments into the cinema of the 1930s.[26] Prévert in particular sought to move away from outright adaptation or theatricalization of dialogue, and looked to privilege the intrinsic capability of film dialogue to essentialize the identity of his protagonists. As Eder suggests,

> In Carné, Prévert found a director whose clarity of vision and ease with actors brought his work to the screen without any compromises; Carné, in turn, had in Prévert a source of characters and story that any director would have craved.[27]

Prévert was born in 1900 in Paris and was an accomplished poet, playwright and painter. By the late 1920s, he began writing poetry and shortly after emerged as a leading member of the Surrealist movement. In 1932 he joined the agitprop *Groupe Octobre*, an ideologically motivated left-wing theatre group that toured factories and political rallies and dramatized current social events to the assembled crowds. He became increasingly involved in cinema, appearing briefly in *L'Atalante* in 1934, and he wrote the screenplay for his brother Pierre's burlesque farce *L'Affaire est dans le sac* in 1932. While some of his other 1930s film collaborations were are now largely forgotten (Marc Allégret's *L'Hôtel du libre échange* [1934], Claude Autant-Lara's *Ciboulette* [1932] and *My Partner Mr Davis* [1934]), Prévert's most important pre-Carné achievement was his deft screenplay for Renoir's *Le Crime de monsieur Lange* (1935). The film typifies the Prévertian style: popular speech, song, proverbs and clichés incorporated into a romantic-pessimistic narrative. A masterpiece of economy and narrative momentum, the film contains the trademark wit and acerbic dialogue that would permeate Carné's later films. The flashback sequences which bookend the narrative, as Valentine recounts Lange's 'crime' to a bar-room jury, anticipate the structural complexities of *Le Jour se lève*, while the character of Batala (Jules Berry) is a clear dry-run for Valentin.

The lucidity of Prévert's writing had impressed Carné after a performance of the former's play *La Bataille de Fontenoy* in 1933. They met in early 1936, and Carné asked Prévert to help him adapt *Prison de velours* as a vehicle for Françoise Rosay. The result, *Jenny*, began the fruitful collaboration that endured up until *La Marie du port* (1950), with the only break being Prévert's absence from *Hôtel du Nord*. His work on *Le Quai des brumes* began to encapsulate fully the 'romantic pessimism' register of Poetic Realism. The dialogue throughout is a perfect counterpoint to the visual depictions of inertia – 'Where are you going?', 'I don't know', 'I'm going your way …' – while the famous interchange between Jean Gabin and Michèle Morgan – 'T'as de beaux yeux, tu sais' ['You've beautiful eyes, you know'] – captures the fleeting ephemerality of love and the ultimate impossibility of its consecration that exemplifies the Carné-Prévert partnership. Their relationship was based around binary constructs – Carné the fatalistic pessimist, Prévert the urgent optimist, Carné embracing 'hyper-formalism and icy classicism', Prévert 'wring[ing] eloquence' and displaying a 'fundamental confidence' in human nature[28] – which fused the poetic and the realistic into a rich romantic fatalism.

Prévert's own poetry is especially revealing of his optimistic view of love and union, and finds echoes in his film scripts. In *Le Jardin*, he writes: 'Thousands of years and thousands more / Would not suffice / To describe / That little second of eternity / Which transpired when you kissed me.'[29] The scene between François and Françoise in the greenhouse in *Le Jour se lève* reflects this impossibility of sustained emotional fulfilment. Elsewhere, Prévert's poems place a great deal of importance on objects, an aspect which resonates within the visual fabric of Carné's Poetic Realist films.[30] Prévert had flirted with the Surrealists in the mid-1920s, and a lyrical brand of Surrealism inflects his 1930s and 1940s collaborations with Carné. This is achieved most explicitly through the way in which the different emotional aspects of individual lives can be represented through objects and the often illogical associations encapsulated within them. Prévert's sensitivity to the poetic consciousness of objects resonates throughout Carné's work: a recurring image in *Drôle de drame* is hundreds of empty milk bottles, and in *Les Visiteurs du soir* (1942) a smashed vase of flowers transforms into a knot of writhing snakes. When Diego (Yves Montand) and Malou (Natalie Nattier) dance together in the workshop in *Les Portes de la nuit* (1946) amidst alabaster plaster casts and one-armed sculptures, Prévert integrates a de Chirico-style Surrealism within an austere narrative framework.[31] Bazin concluded that *Le Jour se lève* is 'all written in verse or at least in prose which is invisibly poetic'.[32] This sustained deployment of a lyrical, highly elegant tone – in which words like 'lilacs', 'mimosas', 'milk' and 'sand' are used to underpin the film's metaphysical register – underlines Prévert's importance in the Carné project. He brings the Poetic to Carné's Realism. Small wonder, then, that Carné would often refer to Prévert as his 'co-author'.

Alexandre Trauner (set designer)

It was perhaps inevitable that Trauner would work with Carné. Not only had both served apprenticeships under another longstanding director-designer team of the 1930s, René Clair and Lazare Meerson, but both also sought to 'schematise the real through elaborate artifice'.[33] Born in Hungary in 1906, Trauner initially trained as a watercolour painter but fled growing anti-Semitism in Budapest and settled in Paris in 1930. He trained under Meerson (whose work with Clair on *Sous les toits de Paris*, *Le Million* (1931) and *À nous la liberté* (1931) defined early 1930s French studio design) and together they instigated many of the visual aspects of Poetic Realism, combining quotidian decor with an accentuated decorative style. As émigrés, both Meerson and Trauner provided cinematic images of Frenchness that combined 'the aesthetic challenge of verisimilitude' and 'the appeal of the exotic discovery'.[34] The dynamic climate of 1930s French filmmaking provided ideal conditions for the émigré set designer, who was able to assimilate personal thematic and visual preoccupations within a receptive, integrationist national culture. Notwithstanding his successful post-war Hollywood collaborations with the likes of Billy Wilder (*The Apartment* – for which he won an Academy Award in 1960 – and *The Private Life of Sherlock Holmes* [1970]), Howard Hawks (*Land of the Pharaohs* [1955]) and John Huston (*The Man Who Would Be King* [1975]), it is Trauner's contribution to French Poetic Realist cinema that remains his abiding legacy. His sets for *Le Quai des brumes* and *Le Jour se lève* in particular combine the quotidian with the poetic, creating 'a paradoxical blend of minutely detailed realism with symbolic, suggestive effects'[35] that best typify the design practices of 1930s French cinema and anticipate the accentuated realism of American post-war *noir*.

Trauner had already worked with Carné on three films. His bustling Limehouse streets and imaginative rendering of Victorian London were an integral part of *Drôle de drame*. He combined a meticulously executed foreground realism with an abstract background one, and used forced perspective to give the sets the illusion of stretching to a vanishing point. This reliance upon perspectival tricks became a characteristic part of Trauner's oeuvre (recall the infinite expanse of the Boulevard du Crime in *Les Enfants du paradis*, or the Kafkaesque anonymity of Jack Lemmon's office in *The Apartment*) and marks Trauner out as one of the great innovators of studio design. Jill Forbes noted how the charm of Trauner's sets was 'the charm of recognition, the pleasure deriving from the fact the physical environment is exactly as the viewer somehow always expected it to be, a second-level recreation'.[36] By maintaining a balance between authentic, documentary-sourced detail and accentuated reality, Trauner created sets 'which tell stories' ['qui dit le drame'].[37] By distilling a visual concept from the thematic and psychological concerns of the screenplay, Trauner's skill was to appropriate realism and then simplify, stylize or accentuate it into an expressive decor.

Maurice Jaubert (composer)

Despite his involvement in many key films of the 1930s, most historical studies of French cinema afford only passing reference to Jaubert, an absence all the more tragic due to his premature death in 1940 during the first months of the Occupation. Previous studies of *Le Jour se lève* have tended to regard the score as minor constituent element, a decision symptomatic of the way a score is usually seen as a post-production addition that sustains mood and keys audience expectations to a narrative development. Yet Jaubert's work on *Le Jour se lève* combines a 'poetic lyricism and playfulness'[38] that is fundamental to the overall understanding and appreciation of the film. Born in 1900, he abandoned an early career as a lawyer to concentrate on music. After graduating from the Nice Conservatoire, he composed a number of chamber and choral works (*Cantate pour le temps pascal* [1936], *Trio Italien* [1936], two ballets (*Le Jour* [1931] and *S.S. Normandie* [1936]), and accompaniments to stage plays (*La Guerre de Troie n'aura pas lieu* [1935]) and silent films (*Nana* [1926] and *Le Petit Chaperon rouge* [1929]). His work throughout 1930s film was equally prolific and influential. Before working with Carné on *Drôle de drame*, *Le Quai des brumes* and *Hôtel du Nord*, he had already composed the haunting scores for Jean Vigo's *Zéro de conduite* (1933) and *L'Atalante* (1934), and the poignant melodies to Clair's early sound film *Quatorze juillet* (1932). His scores were melodic and harmonic, and made innovative use of individual instruments such as the drum, the piccolo and the oboe. Unlike Trauner, who argued that decor should paraphrase the narrative, Jaubert developed scores that would add to the action through a gradual process of accretion. He argued that

> [t]he essence of music is […] rhythm organized temporally. In making it the slave of [dramatic] events or gestures, which, by their nature, do not correspond to a defined rhythm but rather to physiological or psychological reactions […] music is reduced to mere sound.[39]

This explicit juxtaposition of sound and time can be found most readily in the structure of *Le Jour se lève*, in which the percussive rhythmic motifs of Jaubert's score introduce and conclude each of the film's temporal transgressions. By also believing that music should 'convey the internal rhythm of visual imagery',[40] Jaubert approached each score as means of underlining and counterpointing the action.

Throughout his career, Jaubert used music sparingly, to underline an emotion or conclude a scene. Dudley Andrew has written how Jaubert's score for *Le Quai des brumes* displays a relentlessness which acts 'on the body of the film continually and chemically, not unlike the dominant gray of its lighting'.[41] Here, the music is frequently faint and inaudible, as if trying to emerge out of the *grisaille* that envelopes the film's visual and tonal texture. It is a highly innovative approach, as the abstention from redundant musical cues and sentimental background sound permits a deepening of the harmony between the pictorial and the structural. Jaubert felt that music should 'make physically perceptible […] the inner rhythm of the image, without struggling to provide a translation of its content, whether this be emotional, dramatic or poetic'.[42] Accordingly, the sonic architecture of *Le Jour se lève* is characterized by an austerity that directly reflects the melancholy inherent in the *mise-en-scène*.

Curt Courant (cinematographer)

Courant was born in Germany in 1899 and began working on German and Italian silent films as an assistant cameraman. He fled Nazi Germany in 1933 and worked regularly in England and France, where some of his most notable work was for distinguished directors like Fritz Lang (*Frau im Mond* [1929]), Alfred Hitchcock (*The Man Who Knew too Much* [1934]), Max Ophüls (*De Mayerling à Sarajevo* [1940]) and Charlie Chaplin (*Monsieur Verdoux* [1947]). Courant's work in France, as cinematographer for both Renoir's *La Bête humaine* (1938) and *Le Jour se lève*, makes him a major participant in the development of Poetic Realism.

The move towards studio filming and set design in the early 1930s saw a concomitant increase in the importance of expressionist lighting. If the development of the Poetic Realist aesthetic was aided by an effortless manipulation of light and shadow, this was partly due to the ease with which light sources could now be controlled and manipulated. Controlled lighting was an integral indicator of states of mind, and, like the decor, carried a powerful emotional charge. This tradition of expressive lighting in 1930s French cinema was inherited from German Expressionist émigré cinematographers like Courant and Eugen Schüfftan, who recognized the compositional beauty of placing monochromic template lighting onto the decor and who used light as an amplifier of narrative concerns. Gilles Deleuze's description of the use of light in Carné's films as a 'luminous grey which passes through every atmospheric nuance'[43] stands as a collective summation of the visual properties instigated by these émigrés.

Le Jour se lève was the only Carné film that Courant collaborated on (Carné worked with several different cinematographers in the 1930s, such as Schüfftan, Henri Alekan and Armand Thirard), and he made a critical contribution to the film's visual style. His elegant framing, nimble camera movement and lighting decisions on *Le Jour se lève* seal the film's sombre poetic sensibilities. Courant's role was also pedagogic, as he mentored the film's three younger French assistant cinematographers, André Bac, Philippe Agostini and Albert Viguier. Though not listed in the opening credits, Courant initiated a whole range of decorative strategies in the film, such as the use of shadow to sculpt and texture Trauner's designs and the illumination of the steam from a passing train next to Françoise's house. Courant had already lit Jean Gabin on Renoir's *La Bête humaine*, and both films capture the actor in a deeply expressive manner, using mirrors to frame and reflect him, and an omnidirectional light source to define and accentuate objects around him. Courant foregrounds the decor through aggressive spotlighting and crafts a strong psycho-physiological climate in which objects, characters and set design were all shrouded in indeterminacy. As Alastair Phillips states, Courant and other émigré film technicians placed 'the evocation of social atmosphere and detail over the sheer display and artifice of pure spectacle and performance'.[44]

Jean Gabin (François)

[Gabin] has been the ironic or mournful runaway, the unlucky killer, the man who trots waving behind the train, misses the boat, gets entangled with a slut, all this, and yet always worth respecting and worth desiring.[45]

Before *Le Jour se lève* begins, the words 'Jean Gabin dans un film de Marcel Carné' ('Jean Gabin in a Marcel Carné film) are prominently displayed. By 1939, Gabin's 'name-above-the-title' status was so entrenched that he had become France's most popular box-office star. Audience polls conducted by the trade magazine *La Cinématographie française* between 1936 and 1938 ranked Gabin as eleventh, second and most popular film star respectively. By this point too, he had assumed a 'mythic' quality, standing for a whole class of people – the decent, hard-working proletarian labourer struggling against forces that seemed intent on crushing him. Memorably described by André Bazin as 'Oedipus in a cloth cap',[46] Gabin represented a wish-fulfilment figure for the working-class French audience. Many of his 1930s roles were workers – print-setters, soldiers, train-drivers, sand-blasters – and placed a whole class of people at the forefront of cinematic representation. He was the 'common working man whose innate dignity is destroyed by social forces beyond his control',[47] a role he had perfected in the latter half of the 1930s – as the *guinguette* owner in *La Belle Équipe* (1936), destroyed by his partner's jealousy and mistrust, as the train driver driven to murder in *La Bête humaine*, even the genial escaped prisoner-of-war in *La Grande Illusion* (1937), stripped of dignity by the horrors of combat.

Gabin was born Jean-Alexis Moncorgé in Meriel, north of Paris, in 1904. He followed in the footsteps of his cabaret-entertainer parents and became a dancer at the *Folies Bergère*. He played supporting roles in music-hall, operettas and theatre before signing for Pathé-Natan to work on *Chacun sa chance* in 1930. Small supporting roles followed, before Julien Duvivier cast him as the lead in *Maria Chapdelaine* (1934). From this point, his popularity increased exponentially, becoming the quintessential face of the Poetic Realist films of the mid- to late 1930s: *La Bandera* (1935), *La Belle Équipe*, *Gueule d'amour* (1936), *Pépé le Moko* (1937) and the Carné diptych, *Le Quai des brumes* and *Le Jour se lève*. Each of these roles consecrated a body of films in which Gabin played out similar scenarios involving violence, the impossibility of redemptive love, thwarted escape and death. Defining traits could be traced across many of his characters – alienation, helplessness, assertive masculinity, romanticism, a combination of the virulent and the vulnerable – which provided recognizable character coordinates that were modulated or amplified from film to film.

If star persona depends 'on coherence, a neat fit between who we think the star is and the roles he or she assumes',[48] then Gabin is a useful example of the way in which this persona evolves and coheres through a triangular rapport between individual, actor and character. Typical of the star system is how the production process revolves around the star, so that narrative, acting, setting and lighting are all manipulated to enhance the 'star quality'. Susan Hayward writes that the idealized representation of the 1930s working-class male (Gabin being the exemplar) 'has power over his immediate entourage – power to attract, dominate and seduce men and women of his own class'.[49] Appropriately, Gabin had more close-ups than any other actor in French cinema in the 1930s and was usually framed centre screen, functioning as diegetic and non-diegetic figure of identification. *Mise-en-scène* also assisted in strengthening his allure, whether through a band of light on his eyes, or a tracking camera that would follow his movements across rooms or through public spaces.[50] His typicality is also reflected in his acting style, which often resorted to 'straightforwardness and bluntness'[51] to convey typically masculine registers of emotional introversion, silent stoicism, and an aura of sexual potency.[52]

Gabin's film performances were founded on notions of difference and of gestural 'newness'. Whereas the 'theatrical' idiom that he deployed in his earlier film roles was typified by gesticulation and spontaneous movement, Gabin's later performance style was characterized by understatement and an absence of movement. This emphasis on stillness serves a critical role, for any distinctive movement Gabin *does* make becomes exponentially more significant. His work prior to *Le Jour se lève* (most notably for Carné, Renoir and Duvivier) was predicated upon the internalization of rage and the inward playing of intense emotion. There is a sense in several of Gabin's key 1930s roles of a battening down of mood that allows for incremental accretions before an inevitable outburst of emotion (the famous 'explosion de colère' that occurred in several Gabin films of the period, such as *La Grande Illusion* and *Gueule d'amour* became a 'mini-spectacle in [its] own right'[53]). These paroxysms occur on five occasions in *Le Jour se lève* – in the opening moments of the film, when the audience hears but does not see the murder; in the café with Valentin; in Clara's bedroom; most aggressively in his window scene to the crowd below; and in the climactic scene with Valentin. To this day, he looms large in French cinema: from 1981 to 2006, the Prix Jean Gabin was awarded to up-and-coming French actors.

France in the 1930s – the film industry and dominant genres

Traditional approaches to 1930s French film practice incline towards rigid dichotomies. Critics often argue that whereas 1920s French Impressionist and Surrealist cinema had been held up as an example of the medium's potential for dreamy pictorialism and narrative experimentation, the immediate post-talkie era (1928–29) saw French cinema regress to tried-and-tested stories that failed to carry forward the bold graphic techniques bequeathed by the Surrealists, or invoke the strong sense of place that Louis Delluc and Marie Epstein had explored in films like *La Femme de nulle part* (1922) and *Coeur fidèle* (1923). As befits such a regressive discourse, the language used to describe these films is highly normative: writing in 1932, Carné himself bemoaned the recurrence of 'flat vaudeville entertainments [...] grinding out the same pretty stories, incessantly repeating the same tired effects' and denouncing the 'banal, infantile little stories, shopworn entertainments'.[54] Subsequent critics and historians tended to replicate these views. In his influential study of 1930s cinema, *15 ans d'années trente*, Jean-Pierre Jeancolas reaffirmed that 'French films of the 1930s talk too much: they recite tirades already worn out on the stage by one, and sometimes two, generations of actors',[55] while Roy Armes referred to the 'stylistically anonymous canned theatre'[56] aesthetic of the early 1930s. However, it is important to remember that influential directors and canonical films are not always the dominant tendency and should always be analysed alongside their contemporaries. For every Gabin there was a Sacha Guitry or a Fernandel; for every *Le Jour se lève* there was a *Le Roman d'un tricheur* (1936) or a *Le Schpountz* (1938). Poetic Realism may be more intrinsically atmospheric that the more uncinematic 'filmed theatre', but, as Vincendeau maintains, both types of film form 'a representative and informative picture of classical French cinema'.[57] Whereas it is true that much of the French cinema of this period followed distinct genres, it is important not simply to reject *cinéma du samdi soir* (popular cinema) as a retrograde cultural product. The coming of sound certainly introduced a narratives based on literary and theatrical adaptations as well as the transpositions of burlesques and melodramas from stage to screen, but these films, with their critique of French institutions and class systems, their valorization of the working class and their intertwining of various popular modes of entertainment, are all useful texts for interrogating and reframing diverse socio-political and cultural issues in 1930s France. Rather than becoming the dominant mode of film practice that critics are quick to label it, Poetic Realism is but one of a number of different genres and sensibilities located within French 1930s film.

An industry responds

The magnitude of the infrastructural weaknesses within the French film industry during the 1930s has been well documented. Much has been written of the volatility of an industry beset by fragile and vulnerable economic conditions, 'lurching from one crisis to another'.[58] Yet the period 1931–33 had actually been a rather successful period for French cinema. In contrast to other European nations, France had weathered the economic aftermath of the 1929 Wall Street Crash reasonably well. Various factors – heavy industry and plant investment, the establishment of Paris as a hub of creativity, enhanced exhibition and distribution policies, imaginative development of decor practice – created ripe conditions for French sound cinema.

If anything, it was the sheer pace of change – and the industry's inability to adapt to it – throughout the first half of the decade that sowed the seeds for future fragmentation and disorder. There was no centralized administrative body or coherent financing strategies, while uncontrolled foreign imports, failed mergers and high taxation added to the instability. Despite a rapid emergence of new production companies (nearly 450 in the two years from 1933 to 1935 alone), up to a third went bankrupt each year. Following a series of financial scandals, France's two major film companies, Pathé-Natan and Gaumont-Franco-Film-Aubert suffered a similar fate in 1934. Equally debilitating was the withdrawal of American studio Paramount in 1933, which had set up studios in France three years earlier to tap into the newfound enthusiasm for multilingual film production. Once they left, taking resources and personnel back to America, an already brittle industry was further destabilized.

And yet, paradoxically, out of this atomized landscape of 'cultural pessimism and industrial panic',[59] masterpieces were produced, and flourished. The vacuum created in France by the withdrawal and liquidation of major companies meant that those smaller independent production companies that did survive were able to prosper, and by the end of the 1930s were producing as much as ninety per cent of French films. Instead of being compelled by a producer to subscribe to a cost-product analysis, to justify a particular choice of actor, or to adhere to rigid storylines, the industry became more artisanal, whereby directors with a strong personal vision could assemble a team of skilled screenwriters, composers, cinematographers and set designers who each allied themselves to a single vision. Unimpeded by the institutional constraints of earlier studio production practice, they were free to produce more stimulating and challenging work. New funding initiatives were established, and directors found that cooperatives were prepared to finance films.[60]

Textural developments also emerged, such as improvements in lighting and increasingly elaborate studio set designs. These techniques were partially instigated by two types of migration; the industrial migrations of the late 1920s and early 1930s; and the enforced migrations of the mid-1930s. With indus-trial migration, European technicians gravitated to Paris to take advantage of the many networks that had sprouted between France and other European countries throughout the late 1920s. This cross-cultural dissemination was most evident in the relationship between France and Germany, where, for example, the German company Tobis set up a subsidiary studio in Paris to finance prestigious 'French' products such as René Clair's groundbreaking *Sous les toits de Paris*. Similarly, Paramount refurbished the Joinville Studios in Paris in 1930 to facilitate the production of multilingual films that could be shot in a number of different languages simultaneously and be exported across the continent. The strategy was vocational as well as financial, as actors, directors, cameramen and other technicians from around Europe met, shared expertise and disseminated ideas in Paris. This criss-crossing of personnel, capital and equipment provided a service that 'could enhance rather than subvert the needs of the French industry at a crucial period of transition in its cultural practice'.[61]

The second wave of immigration was politically motivated. With the accession to power of the Nazis in Germany and political unrest across Eastern Europe, many technicians left for Paris. Both Curt Courant and Alexandre Trauner were part of this immigrant wave and they, along with others, imported conspicuous visual and stylistic techniques to France's developing sound cinema. Through this osmosis and 'flux and exchange',[62] a visual 'newness' was injected into French cinema. Innovative lighting, decor and cinematographic trends permeated studio practice, helping to introduce a consistency of thematic and formal elements. Such transnational hybridity allowed psychology and character to be externalized more effectively than ever before.

Different types of films

The impact of sound correlates to the types of films being made at this time. Its arrival resembled 'a new chemical which interacted violently with pre-existing practices'[63] and had several financial and aesthetic consequences, not the least of which was the pleasure film audiences now took in hearing French spoken or sung. Sound conversion pushed costs up, with the result that French cinema tended to abandon the narrative experimentations of the 1920s in favour of financing products that would appeal to a much wider public. Sound also introduced a cinema in which dialogue and song could play a central role. This in part explains the rise of 'filmed theatre', ready-made scripts that could be cheaply made, broadly marketed and packaged as a distinctive French product.

While there was no single common paradigm encompassing 1930s French cinema, three types of film dominated, each connected to sound. The first, 'filmed theatre', was the principal genre of this period and borrowed from a number of sources (boulevard comedies, *café-théâtre*, cabaret, *comique troupier*), while the second, 'musical fantasy', encompassed vaudeville, musicals and operettas. Frequent impromptu song and dance routines would be inserted into these films, heralding a popular aesthetic that helped to 'shore up a specifically French cinema in the face of Hollywood'.[64] Despite having broad popular appeal with audiences, these are the films routinely denounced by critics has having little or no aesthetic worth. In fact, they are crucial in elucidating the ways in which the industry responded to financial and structural problems by mass-producing films that foregrounded working-class communities and popular modes of entertainment. The memorable outbursts of spontaneous singing by Fernandel in the military comedy *Ignace* (1937) and Jean Gabin in *La Belle Équipe* were 'loosely connected and sometimes barely justified moments of pure spectacle',[65] and clearly highlighted the way that idioms of theatricality and self-reflexivity had been progressively incorporated into French sound cinema through the medium of song. Actors like Fernandel and Gabin were enormously popular, not least because they embodied the community spirit and the sense of freedom and spontaneity in these popular films. The third trend was 'realist cinema', which can in turn be subdivided into two strands. The first, 'social realism', was epitomized by some of the films of Jean Renoir.[66] These films – *Toni* (1934), *Le Crime de monsieur Lange* (1935), *La Vie est à nous* (1936) – stressed the authentic and the 'real', and usually centred on the working class within a specific environment. They were characterized by a diversity of setting and tone, fluid camera movements, deep-focus photography and authentic *mise-en-scène*, and depicted a broad panorama of French society. The second subdivision was 'Poetic Realism', and it is to this that we now turn.

Poetic Realism

When I paint a tree, I make everybody ill at ease. That's because there is something or someone hidden behind that tree. I paint those things hidden behind things. For me, a swimmer has already drowned. (Michel Krauss [Robert Le Vigan], in *Le Quai des brumes*)

Leaf through any book on French cinema and the term 'Poetic Realism' will be prominently displayed. *Le Jour se lève* is the culmination of a filmmaking praxis and visual style that flourished throughout the 1930s and has now come to represent French Golden Age cinema. Its most haunting images can be found on the frontispieces of most French cinema histories, it is often deemed (erroneously) representative of the dominant mode of French film practice in the 1930s and it is regarded as the starting point of other broader evolutions in the development of a specifically French national cinema.

Edward Baron Turk describes Poetic Realism as 'that brand of cinema which aims to illuminate the invisible lying within the normally visible world'.[67] Indeed, as Robert Le Vigan's tortured artist reiterates in *Le Quai des brumes*, all is not as it first appears in Poetic Realism. The term was first applied to film in 1934 in a review of Pierre Chenal's film *La Rue sans nom*, but most trade papers and journals in the 1930s tended to use the term '*film d'atmosphère*' to classify those dark, atmospheric French films of the mid- to late 1930s that were a counterpoint to the theatrical and literary adaptations, '*diversion*' films, and popular genres of the time. There is a lack of consensus over its exact definition, time period, adherents and representative corpus. Generally speaking, Poetic Realism is a post-World War II critical construct that is best defined as 'pessimistic urban dramas, usually set in Paris [...] in working class settings, with doomed romantic narratives often tinged with criminality'.[68]

In 1949, Georges Sadoul detected in Poetic Realism a rich cultural tradition, notably 'the influence of Zola's literary naturalism [and] the input of René Clair and Jean Vigo and [...] Marcel Pagnol'.[69] He also noted how, after 1937, a darker, more pessimistic strain of Poetic Realism developed, which combined the visual influences of German Expressionism and the *Kammerspielfilm* to produce films exemplified by *Le Jour se lève*. Like Zola, Poetic Realism was intent on unmasking the seamier side of life through poetic discourse which aestheticized the sordid and relied upon a fully documented representation of a familiar environment and the recurrence of stock characters. The reference to Marcel Pagnol is also crucial, not least because both Poetic Realism and Pagnol's more melodramatic register relied upon the 'intentionality of the decor',[70] and a strong visual and narrative sense established by iconography, cast and performances. This tight interweaving of character, dialogue and *mise-en-scène* in Pagnol's *Merlusse* (1935), *César* (1936) and *La Femme du boulanger* (1938) is mirrored in Carné's 1930s films. Sadoul also mentions avant-garde films like Epstein's *La Belle Nivernaise* (1923) and Delluc's *Fièvre* (1921) as strong pictorial influences, as well as documentaries by Vigo, Georges Lacombe and Jean Dréville that explored the interaction between milieu and character that Poetic Realism would develop in a more systematic way.

Subsequent attempts to define Poetic Realism broadly followed Sadoul's initial methodology. Jean Mitry (1980) saw it as 'a toned-down Expressionism inserted into the norms and conditions of an immediate real'.[71] Whereas Sadoul looked within France for Poetic Realism's contexts, Mitry identified its transnational facets, linking it to D.W. Griffith's *Broken Blossoms* (1919), Joseph von Sternberg's *The Blue Angel* (1930) and Fritz Lang's *M* (1931). He argued that Poetic Realism displayed a degree of studio-bound formal stylization that was most manifestly visualized through the decor. This emphasis on the primacy of set design – protagonists are 'determined by the milieu which surrounded them'[72] – is an approach that has become increasingly useful, and one that we shall look at in more detail in the next chapter.

Later studies of 1930s cinema by Chirat (1983) and Lagny et al. (1986) omit the term Poetic Realism completely, implicitly recognizing its troublesome status, while Armes (1985) and Williams (1992) use the term as a generic label for any 1930s French film that displays a strong visual style and takes place in an atmospheric milieu.[73] More recently, Andrew (1995), Andrew and Ungar (2005), Crisp (2002) and Vincendeau (2004) have departed from an auteurist approach and instead place set designers, cinematographers and actors at the heart of the evolutionary process of Poetic Realism. All regard it as constitutive of a far more coherent national cinema than had previously been conceptualized. For instance, Andrew classifies Poetic Realism as an *optique*, 'a sensibility, a function, and a mode of address'.[74] The *optique* indicates the finite series of cinematic possibilities open to a filmmaker at a given time that can be defined as the recurrence of a set of themes, a unified visual tone, audience appeal, socio-cultural function and the spectatorial experience offered by Poetic Realism. By moving beyond wholly text-based interpretations of Poetic Realism, Andrew's notion of the *optique* permits a deeper, more composite examination of the triangular relationship between the films, their contemporaneous audience and their historical context.[75] *Le Jour se lève* in this context aims to 'provide an experience so immediate that the spectators never think to admire the expression that touches [them] to the bone'.[76]

It is worth addressing three other important socio-cultural aspects of Poetic Realism: the photographic, the literary and cultural representations of the working class. The emphasis on the photographic resonates with the visual imperatives of Poetic Realism: Alastair Phillips has written of 1930s French realist cinema's 'almost ethnographic interest in the listing, picturing and recording the ordinary world of the city'.[77] These themes ran strongly through the work of the Hungarian émigré photographer Brassaï, who throughout the 1930s took thousands of photographs of traditionally working-class areas of Paris. Brassaï's technique involved avoiding the immediate light of lamp posts and instead diffusing it through trees and allowing it to reflect on rainy streets. The similarities between Brassaï's photography and the visual *topoi* of Poetic Realism is striking: photographs like *Nighthawks* (in which city employees empty a cesspit) and the grainy quality of *Passers-By in the Rain* or *The Stairs* could have been taken as still frames from *Le Quai des brumes* or *Le Jour se lève*. Brassaï, along with his contemporaries Eugène Atget, Henri Cartier-Bresson and André Kertész, provides visual echoes of the haunting quality of the city streets that Trauner refabricated in his most memorable sets. Poetic Realism ushered into French cinema a heightened awareness of space and a sensibility for atmosphere. Carné, Vigo, Chenal and Renoir, like Brassaï and Atget, each resembled 'the furtive curiosity of the stalker'.[78] By perpetuating the legacy of films such as *Fièvre* and *La Femme de nulle part* that had turned industrial wildernesses and deserted streets into atmospheric depictions of urban space, the new directors privileged atmosphere, transmuting the urban mundane into the material of poetry.

The written word was equally decisive in the development of Poetic Realism. The 1930s was a dynamic time for French literary culture, due to a publishing boom at Gallimard and Flammarion and the emerging cultural policy of the French Communist Party. Just as important was the publication of Henri Poulaille's 1930 manifesto *Nouvel âge littéraire*, which called for the creation of proletarian and populist literature. Populism has been described as 'an earnest, avowedly middlebrow reaction to the verbal acrobatics of the avant-garde'[79] and as a literary phenomenon sought to capture the ambience of working-class life. Whereas previous representations of Paris had been primarily filtered through middle-class writers like Victor Hugo, new populist writers emerged who were ideal chroniclers of the social and political transformations affecting French urban society. This democratization of an existing traditional culture enabled the likes of Eugène Dabit, Jules Romains, Marcel Aymé, Pierre Mac Orlan and Francis Carco to become increasingly influential, while the ongoing popularity of Georges Simenon's socially inflected crime fiction also forged a link with Poetic Realism's preoccupations with clear class parameters, criminal figures and the underworld milieu (first illustrated in Renoir's suitably murky 1932 adaptation of Simenon's *La Nuit du Carrefour*, and later revisited by Carné, Gabin and Trauner in their 1950 version of *La Marie du port*).

Populism was also an ideological formulation that proposed placing the working class at the forefront of cultural achievement. Carné's own role in the development of this ideological aspect was crucial. While a critic and journalist at *Cinémagazine* in the late 1920s, he published two influential articles that attempted to map out the route that French sound cinema should follow. The first, 'La caméra, personnage du drame' ['The Camera as Dramatic Actor'],[80] invoked an admiration of F.W. Murnau, whose deployment of the tracking shot in *Sunrise* (1927) had initiated a new relationship between actors and decor and who, Carné felt, brought a vitality to his urban settings. The second, 'Quand le cinéma descendra-t-il dans la rue?' ['When Will the Cinema go out onto the Street?'],[81] developed these themes, suggesting that the urban environment and the *petit peuple* ought to be important presences in French cinema. Carné also wrote that filmmakers needed to look at popular novelists like Dabit and Romains and see how they 'study certain Parisian *quartiers* and seize the hidden spirit under the familiar facade of those streets'.[82] He highlighted the visuality of their novels and applauded their grasp of traditional urban topographies. That several Poetic Realist films (*La Rue sans nom*, *Gueule d'amour* and *Hôtel du Nord*) were adapted from French populist novels shows how far these rich atmospheric texts found a visual cognate on film. To visualize the life of the working class required an expressive decor in which popular Paris and the intermingling of class, gender and the heterogeneity of the *quartier* could be represented. The articles were urgent tracts calling for a cinema sensitive to ordinary people's daily lives, and as such anticipated debates about location shooting and cinematic spontaneity put forward by the *Cahiers du cinéma* group in the mid-1950s. Carné suggests that the new reality sound cinema was seeking to capture was linked to a conscious desire to create a more democratic cinema that would combine populism and underlying social comment to celebrate and ennoble the working class.

An interesting intersection between the photographic and the literary should be flagged up here. Carné, who never regarded himself as a Poetic Realist filmmaker, preferred to align himself with the designation *fantastique social*.[83] This aesthetic, based upon the 'subtle defamiliarization of contemporary reality in order to create an atmosphere of fear or disquiet',[84] derives primarily from the French popular novelist Pierre Mac Orlan. Novels like *Sous la lumière froide*, *La Tradition de minuit* and *Quartier réservé* were characterized by a documentary-style proximity to the street and an ability to pictorialize inner emotions. His subject matter, like Brassaï's photographs of Paris, evokes the iconography of Poetic Realism: dark alleyways, shadows, wet paving stones and isolated street lamps. This combination of surface authenticity underpinned by a 'fantastic' ambiance is inherently cinematic, not least in the way the mysterious nature of contemporary reality can be captured through expressionistic lighting and set design. But Mac Orlan's subject matter is also inherently photographic – a juncture he himself reinforced when he wrote the foreword to a 1934 collection of photographs entitled *Paris vu par André Kertész*. Mac Orlan described the photographer's sensibility as an 'anxiety generated by a fantastic element of the street' and the interpretation of 'secret elements of shadow and light, so that others can draw fictional situations from them'.[85] The conjunction between photography, literature and cinema is fully crystallized in Carné's two films before *Le Jour se lève*. *Le Quai des brumes* is an adaptation of Mac Orlan's novel, corresponding closely to a reality that is essentially *fantastique* and unsettling, while *Hôtel du Nord* restages actual photographs from Kertész's collection and integrates their registers of melancholy and transience into its Poetic Realist *mise-en-scène*.

Finally, both the photographic and the literary aspects of Poetic Realism were fundamental in the evolution of the third aspect: the cultural representation of the working class. By 1939, milieu, behaviour, gesture and language had been accurately represented in several films to provide an idealized version of the proletariat. In 1930, René Clair's *Sous les toits de Paris* ushered in a vital era of populist filmmaking that used song, identifiable spaces and an optimistic depiction of the working class as a means of exploring socio-historical trends and changes. The film (as well as others by Clair, such as *Le Million* and *Quatorze juillet*) valorized a specifically Parisian working-class community and fostered a deep sense of warmth and fraternity. The depiction of working-class values became *de rigueur* throughout the decade. This was achieved in a variety of ways: the depiction of workplaces, notably in *L'Atalante*, *La Bête humaine* and *Le Jour se lève*, linguistic diversity (Bazin regarded the Marseille patois in Pagnol's *Marius-Fanny-César* trilogy not as 'a touch of local colour' but 'the accent of […] realism'[86]), the working class at play in *guinguettes*, *bals musettes* and cafés, the tight bonds of camaraderie that are valorized or critiqued accordingly; in short, the internal topography of French populist cinema, with its class fraternity and community solidarity, was imagined on-screen as a way of targeting spectators and provided them with relevant and recognizable images of themselves.

Poetic Realism became such a dominant trend in critical views of French film because it provided a highly 'international' and exportable version of French national cinema. This was due in part to circumstances both industrial (no French film exports from 1940–45 meant that Poetic Realism was frozen by foreign critics into 'a single, solid, and dazzling block'[87] that became disproportionately representative of pre-war France) and aesthetic (Poetic Realism's visual exquisiteness – set design, lighting, cinematography – travelled better than dialogue-heavy adaptations). The cultural prestige of Poetic Realism was also strengthened by canny foreign distributors who capitalized on the success of French films in the late 1930s on the international awards circuit. *Le Quai des brumes* had already won the best director's prize at the Venice Film Festival, and even though *La Kermesse héroïque, Mayerling, La Grande Illusion, Regain* and *La Femme du boulanger* (which had each carried off the New York Critics Prize for Best Foreign Film in consecutive years from 1935 to 1938) were not examples of Poetic Realism, these successes were all framed as something 'not-quite-Hollywood', the culmination of a mature, poetic visual and narrative style that was recognizably French. Finally, as we shall explore in Chapter 4, clear links between French Poetic Realism and American *film noir* account for Poetic Realism's historiographical pre-eminence. Post-war critics argued that a pre-war European vision of fatalism and unstable gender and class relations had been reworked into an American context. David Thomson's description of Poetic Realism as a 'subdued prediction of film noir – *film gris*'[88] suggests the extent to which the visual codes of films like *Le Jour se lève* had been grafted onto American *noir*.

Filming *Le Jour se lève*

After the premiere of *Hôtel du Nord* in mid-December 1938, Carné and Prévert began working on another collaboration, the gangster film *La Rue des vertus*. They hoped to reunite the same personnel from *Le Quai des brumes*, which had proved to be such a financial and critical success. They had already begun sketching outlines and potential designs, when Jacques Viot, a Montmartre art dealer and Carné's neighbour, presented the director with a three-page synopsis for a film similar in visual style to *La Rue des vertus*, and written expressly for Jean Gabin. It was the film's narrative structure that most appealed to Carné – a complex flashback configuration that marked a radical departure from current storytelling trends. Carné consequently persuaded producer Pierre Frogerais to substitute *Le Jour se lève* for the *La Rue des vertus* and spent three weeks with Prévert in

Fontainebleau developing Viot's treatment. Gabin, Arletty and Jules Berry had already been contracted to the initial film, and so the transition from one project to another was relatively fluid.

Production began at Billancourt, the large studio complex on the outskirts of Paris, on 6 February 1939.[89] As if to attest to the importance of the apartment block within the narrative, it was constructed (along with the town square and intersection) at a size of 7800 m² and Carné employed 200 extras. It was a rather troublesome shoot, with the main problems centring, not surprisingly, on the construction of and manoeuvring around the apartment block. Trauner has frequently recounted how he had to persuade the producers of the film to provide him with more money to build a fifth floor.[90] This balancing act between the exigencies of the story and financial imperatives serves as a useful rejoinder to debates about artistic freedom reined in by economic pragmatism that echoed throughout the decade. Gabin was frequently annoyed at the intricacies of the decor, whose complex four-walled structure meant that actors and crew had to crawl inside the set, rather than enter through the usual open 'fourth wall' of a three-sided structure.

Le Jour se lève's worldview chimes with what Stanley Hoffman has called France's 'stalemated society' (la société bloquée) in which internal paralysis and decline in the 1930s was matched by an increasing powerlessness in external affairs.[91] Certainly, it was filmed against a backdrop of immense social and political turbulence in France, namely the aftermath of the Munich Agreement, that disastrous excursion by British Prime Minister Neville Chamberlain and French head Edouard Daladier to meet Hitler and effectively back out of their obligations to defend Czechoslovakia in the event of conflict. Their trans-European policy of appeasement all but guaranteed the outbreak of World War II a year later. Hence, intuitive parallels between François's fate and the strains of tragedy and pessimism running through the film and French attitudes in the lead-up to World War II, 'awaiting defeat with mesmerised passivity',[92] have frequently been drawn. More generally, Poetic Realist films are often discussed within the same barometrical parameters; namely, works like La Belle Équipe, Le Quai des brumes and Le Jour se lève each chart the rise and fall of optimism engendered by the 1936 Popular Front government, its subsequent collapse and the impending war. These films supposedly articulate the malaise afflicting France, and the petty gangsters, abject paternal figures and thwarted escapees in Le Quai des brumes seem apt allegorical figures for a nation struggling to come to terms with the collapse of the Popular Front and the remilitarization of the Rhineland. Similarly, Le Jour se lève is often perceived as being finely tuned to the current states of affairs, standing as an 'offspring of national crisis, turmoil, and frustration'.[93] We shall examine these knotty, though not entirely unhelpful, 'reflectionist' approaches in more detail in Chapter 3, but given the national climate of uncertainty in mid-1939, it is clear that the film's screenplay and tonal qualities were inflected by the politics of the day. When *Le Jour se lève* was eventually released in June 1939, Carné could scarcely have wished for a more opportune confluence of events – the film's compositional, visual, decorative and performance aspects were all prominently discussed (sometimes begrudgingly, often hostilely), while its pregnant air of melancholy captured the zeitgeist in a highly revealing but ultimately problematic way. Carné and his team each contributed to the film's aesthetics of despair, and their individual accomplishments were crucial. With this in mind, it is time to turn to the film.

Notes

1   Edward Baron Turk, *Child of Paradise: Marcel Carné and the Golden Age of French Cinema* (Cambridge, MA, and London: Harvard University Press, 1989), p. 176.

2   Jean Mitry, *Histoire du cinéma: Art et industrie*, 5 vols (Paris: Jean-Pierre Delarge, 1980), vol. 4: *1930–40*, p. 342.

3   Paul Rotha, *The Film till Now: A Survey of World Cinema* (London: Vision Press, 1949), p. 295.

4   Jill Forbes, *Les Enfants du paradis* (BFI: London, 1997), p. 27.

5   Ibid., p. 44.

6   Jean-Pierre Jeancolas, 'Beneath the despair, the show goes on: Marcel Carné's *Les Enfants du paradis* (1943–5)', trans. Marianne Johnson, in Susan Hayward and Ginette Vincendeau (eds), *French Film: Texts and Contexts*, 2nd edn (London and New York: Routledge, 2000), p. 79.

7   Tim Bergfelder, Sue Harris and Sarah Street, *Film Architecture and the Transnational Imagination: Set Design in 1930s European Cinema* (Amsterdam: Amsterdam University Press, 2007), p. 71.

8   Roy Armes, *French Cinema* (London: Secker and Warburg, 1985), p. 91.

9   David Thomson, *The New Biographical Dictionary of Film* (London: Little, Brown, 2003), p. 136.

10   André Bazin, 'The disincarnation of Carné', in Mary Lea Bandy (ed.), *Rediscovering French Film* (New York: The Museum of Modern Art, 1983), p. 131.

11   Jean-Louis Barrault recalls how Carné's 'meticulousness in setting up shots was so excessive that many of us became a bit irritated' (cited in Turk, *Child of Paradise*, p. 56).

12   Marcel Carné, *La Vie à belles dents* (Paris: Pierre Belfond, 1989), p. 30.

13   From the documentary film *Marcel Carné – Ma vie à l'écran*, dir. Jean-Denis Bonan, 1993.

14   Turk, *Child of Paradise*, p. 26.

15   Raymond Borde, '"The Golden Age": French cinema of the '30s', trans. Catherine A. Surowiec, in Bandy (ed.), *Rediscovering French Film*, p. 67.

16   Turk, *Child of Paradise*, p. 89.

17   Allen Thiher, *The Cinematic Muse: Critical Studies in the History of French Cinema* (Columbia and London: University of Missouri Press, 1979), p. 115.

18   Turk, *Child of Paradise*, p. 116.

19   The film was adapted from the novel by Jean Aurenche and the dialogue was provided by Henri Jeanson. It was Jeanson's idea to develop the characters played by Arletty and Louis Jouvet, who were only peripheral figures in the original novel.

20   A genre of films produced in Germany during the early 1920s that drew on the conventions of contemporary German theatre. Storylines were simplified down to an almost instinctual level and were characterized by claustrophobic settings, strict unity of time and place, the use of unusual camera angles, and a stylized *mise-en-scène*.

21   Hélène Climent-Oms, 'Carné parle', *Cahiers de la cinémathèque* 5 (Winter 1972), p. 36.

22   Carné recognized the impact both Murnau and Lang had had upon his visual style. See ibid., pp. 35–6.

23   Bruce Eder has argued that the closeness of their relationship resembles that of Michael Powell and Emeric Pressburger, not least because both teams created 'worthwhile movies that bore little resemblance to their source material' ('Carné and Prévert', <www. criterionco.com/asp/in_focus_essay.asp?id=9&eid=194> (accessed 1 February 2006).

24   In François Truffaut's review of Carné's '*Le Pays d'où je viens*', *Arts; lettres; spectacles*, 31 October–6 November 1956, p. 3.

25   Armes, *French Cinema*, p. 85.

26   Narrowly elected in May 1936, this left-wing coalition attempted to reverse 'the conservative programme of previous years: instead of giving priority to the economic sector and attempting to balance the budget by reducing expenditure, [it] proposed a series of social reforms involving significant public sector expenditure – the dole, public works, agricultural subsidies, and above all the reduction of the working week to forty hours – intending that these social measures should in turn trigger an economic recovery'. Colin Crisp, *The Classic French Cinema 1930–1960* (Bloomington: Indiana University Press, 1993), p. 4.

27   Eder, 'Carné and Prévert'.

28   Turk, *Child of Paradise*, p. 54.

29   Jacques Prévert, 'Le jardin', *Paroles* (Paris: Gallimard, 1949), p. 233.

30   See Claire Blakeway's *Jacques Prévert: Popular French Theatre and Cinema* (London: Associated University Presses, 1990), p. 29. Blakeway suggests that the Surrealist preoccupation with beautiful and banal juxtapostions dates back to Baudelaire's *Tableaux parisiens*, thus reinforcing the Romantic poetic tradition of seeing objects as transcendent symbols of a higher reality.

31   This use of mannequins in claustrophobic spaces was a clear link back to de Chirico and Carrà's 'Pittura Metafisica' movement of the early 1910s, which, itself an early precursor to Surrealism, used disconnected and mysterious images to forge new and magical atmospheres.

32   Bazin, 'The disincarnation of Carné', p. 12.

33   Turk, *Child of Paradise*, p. 90.

34   Bergfelder, Harris and Street, *Film Architecture and the Transnational Imagination*, p. 64.

35   Sandy Flitterman-Lewis, *To Desire Differently: Feminism and the French Cinema* (Urbana and Chicago: University of Illinois Press, 1990), p. 173.

36   Forbes, *Les Enfants du paradis*, p. 21.

37   Trauner, in Douchet, Jean and Gilles Nadeau, *Paris cinéma: Une ville vue par le cinéma de 1895 à nos jours* (Paris: Éditions du Mars, 1987), p. 127.

38   Catherine A. Surowiec, 'Maurice Jaubert: Poet of music', in *Rediscovering French Film*, p. 87.

39   Jaubert, in Turk, *Child of Paradise*, p. 153.

40   André Bazin, 'Jaubert et le cinéma français', in *Le Cinéma français de la libération à la Nouvelle Vague (1945–1958)*, comp. Jean Narboni (Paris: Petite Bibliothèque des Cahiers du cinéma, 1998), p. 316.

41   Dudley Andrew, *Mists of Regret: Culture and Sensibility in Classic French Film* (Princeton, NJ: Princeton University Press, 1995), p. 270.

42 Jaubert, 'Music on the screen', in Charles Davy (ed.), *Footnotes to the Film* (London: Lovat Dickson Ltd, 1938), p. 109.

43 Gilles Deleuze, *Cinema 2: The Time Image* (London: Continuum, 2005), p. 47.

44 Alastair Phillips, 'Migration and exile in the classical period', in Michael Temple and Michael Witt (eds), *The French Cinema Book* (London: BFI, 2004), p. 108.

45 Dilys Powell, 'Since 1939', repr. in Christopher Cook (ed.), *The Dilys Powell Film Reader* (Manchester: Carcanet, 1991), p. 369.

46 André Bazin, '*Le Jour se lève*', repr. in *Le Cinéma français*, p. 88.

47 Turk, *Child of Paradise*, p. 159.

48 Manohla Dargis, 'Ghost in the machine', *Sight & Sound* (July 2000), p. 20.

49 Susan Hayward, *French National Cinema*, 2nd edn (London: Routledge, 2005), p. 173.

50 See Claude Gauther and Ginette Vincendeau, *Jean Gabin: Anatomie d'un mythe* (Paris: Nathan, 1993), p. 123–5.

51 Rémi Fournier Lanzoni, *French Cinema: From Its Beginnings to the Present* (New York: Continuum, 2004), p. 77.

52 It was seeing Gabin in *Le Jour se lève* that convinced Michael Caine to become an actor: '[Gabin] featured everything that I thought could hold me back: fair hair, a big nose and a small mouth […] He was the biggest star in France, so everything was now possible'. Michael Caine, *What's It All About?* (London: Century, 1992), p. 39.

53 Ginette Vincendeau, *Stars and Stardom in French Cinema* (London and New York: Continuum, 2000), p. 73. It is often said that Gabin cannily inserted an 'outburst of anger' into each of his contracts. This is incorrect, although, says Bazin, 'it deserves to be true' (Bazin, '*Le Jour se lève*', p. 97).

54 Marcel Carné, 'Le cinéma et le monde', *Cinémagazine* 12 (November 1932).

55 Jean-Pierre Jeancolas, *Le Cinéma des français: 15 ans d'années trente (1929–1944)* (Paris: Nouveau monde, 2005), p. 129.

56 Armes, *French Cinema*, p. 71.

57 Ginette Vincendeau, 'The art of spectacle: the aesthetics of classical French cinema', in Temple and Witt, *The French Cinema Book*, p. 138.

58 Colin Crisp, 'Anarchy and order in the classic film industry', in Temple and Witt, *The French Cinema Book*, p. 118.

59 Michael Temple and Michael Witt, 'Introduction 1930–60: classicism and conflict', in Temple and Witt, *The French Cinema Book*, p. 95.

60 The most high-profile ventures were *La Vie est à nous* (1936, Renoir) for the Communist Party, *La Marseillaise* (1937, Renoir) for the Confédération Nationale du Travail (CNT) and *Golgotha* (1935, Duvivier), *L'Appel du silence* (1936, Poirier) and *Thérèse Martin* (1938, de Canonge) for the Catholic Church.

61 Phillips, 'Migration and exile in the classical period', p. 106.

62 Ibid.

63 Crisp, *Classic French Cinema 1930–1960*, p. 108.

64 Vincendeau, 'The art of spectacle: the aesthetics of classical French cinema', p. 141.

65 Ibid., p. 140.

66 It is worth remembering that Renoir had already made several vaudeville and boulevard play adaptations by the mid-1930s, such as *Tire-au-flanc* (1928) et *On purge bébé* (1931).

67 Turk, *Child of Paradise*, p. 102.

68 Ginette Vincendeau, *The Companion to French Cinema* (London: BFI and Cassell, 1996), pp. 115–16.

69 Georges Sadoul, *Histoire du cinéma mondial des origines à nos jours* (Paris: Flammarion, 1949), p. 274.

70 Hayward, *French National Cinema*, p. 172.

71 Mitry, *Histoire du cinéma*, p. 292.

72 Ibid.

73 The abiding paradox of the Poetic Realist corpus is that it was in no way representative

of the dominant mode of filmmaking in the 1930s. For example, Roy Armes has shown that 25 per cent of all French films made between 1936–38 (historically perceived as Poetic Realism's apotheosis) were the product of just ten directors, and, of those, only Pierre Chenal and *Crime et châtiment* could be classified as a film heavily imbued with the Poetic Realist aesthetic. Like all critically acclaimed cinematic movements (one thinks of the French *cinéma du look* or 1960s English 'kitchen sink' social realism), these films constitute the exception rather than the rule. See 'The paradoxes of French realism', in Armes, *French Cinema*, pp. 86–108.

74   Andrew, *Mists of Regret*, p. 25.

75   Alan Williams proposes the following catalogue of the key Poetic Realist films: *La Rue sans nom* (Chenal, 1933), *Le Grand Jeu* (Feyder, 1934), *Crime et châtiment* (Chenal, 1935), *Pension Mimosas* (Feyder, 1935), *Jenny* (Carné, 1936), *Pépé le Moko* (Duvivier, 1937), *La Belle Équipe* (Duvivier, 1936), *Gueule d'amour* (Grémillon, 1937), *L'Alibi* (Chenal, 1937), *Hôtel du Nord* (Carné, 1938), *Le Quai des brumes* (Carné, 1938), *La Bête humaine* (Renoir, 1938), *Le Jour se lève* (Carné, 1939), *Le Dernier Tournant* (Chenal, 1939), *Menaces* (Gréville, 1939) and *Remorques* (Grémillon, 1939–41), in *Republic of Images: A History of French Filmmaking* (Cambridge, MA, and London: Harvard University Press, 1992), p. 419.

76   Andrew, *Mists of Regret*, p. 320.

77   Alastair Phillips, 'The camera goes down the streets: *Dans les rues* (Victor Trivas, 1933) and the Paris of the German émigrés', *Modern and Contemporary France* 8/3 (2000), p. 330.

78   Gaby Wood, 'Seeing in the dark', *Guardian Weekend* (15 July 2000), p. 14.

79   Turk, *Child of Paradise*, p. 130.

80   Marcel Carné, 'La caméra, personnage du drame', *Cinémagazine* (12 July 1929), repr. in Rober Chazal, *Marcel Carné* (Paris: Seghers, 1965), pp. 87–99.

81   Marcel Carné, 'Quand le cinéma descendra-t-il dans la rue?', *Cinémagazine* (November 1933), repr. in Chazal, *Marcel Carné*, pp. 94–6.

82   Ibid., p. 96.

83   Carné certainly felt more at ease with the label. See Climent-Oms, 'Carné parle'.

84   Janette Kay Bayles, 'Figuring the abject: politics, aesthetics and the crisis of national identity in interwar French literature and cinema' (unpublished doctoral dissertation, University of Iowa, 1999), p. 154.

85   Pierre Mac Orlan, *Masques sur mesure* (Paris: Gallimard, 1965), p. 27.

86   André Bazin, 'The Pagnol case', in Mary Lea Bandy (ed.), *Rediscovering French Film* (New York: Museum of Modern Art, 1983), p. 92.

87   Andrew, *Mists of Regret*, p. 14.

88   David Thomson, 'The art of the art director', *American Film* 2/4 (1977), p. 17.

89   The Avenue Le Jour Se Lève remains today in the Parisian commune of Boulogne-Billancourt in homage to the film.

90   See Michel Ciment and Isabelle Jordan, 'Entretien avec Alexandre Trauner (1)', *Positif* 223 (October 1979), pp. 15–16.

91   Hoffmann notes that between 1919 and 1939, France had forty-two governments lasting on average only six months at a time. See Hoffmann, Stanley, *La Société bloquée* (Paris: Le Seuil, 1970).

92   Philip Kemp, 'Le Jour se lève', <http://www.filmreference.com/Films-Im-Le/Le-Jour-se-L-ve.html> (accessed 1 March 2009).

93   Turk, *Child of Paradise*, p. 152.

2 Structure, Set Design, Style

Memory [...] is one of the concepts inscribed in flashbacks. Memory surges forth, it strengthens or protects or it repeats and haunts. (Maureen Turim)[1]

Atmosphère! Atmosphère! (Raymonde [Arletty], in *Hôtel du Nord*)

To examine the visual and structural elements of *Le Jour se lève* is to appreciate the ultimate sublimation of the aesthetic and narrative sensibilities of Poetic Realism. The film employs a range of stylistic tropes that serve the demands of the screenplay and contribute to the overall look of the film. Before examining the film in more detail, I will place *Le Jour se lève* within a specific cinematic tradition. Leo Braudy has argued that there is a dichotomy in classical cinema which governs how films present the visible world: films are either *open* or *closed*. In an open film, 'the world of the film is a momentary frame around an ongoing reality'; in a closed one 'the world of the film is the only thing that exists'.[2] The open style relies particularly on the pictorial; the closed form on the theatrical, and both modalities involve different ways of seeing the world and different ways of experiencing and feeling it. The principal differences can be summarized as follows:

OPEN FILM	CLOSED FILM
The frame is like a window, offering a privileged view to a world of which there exists multiple views	Everything is determined by a larger design and has a formal function
There is a dynamic visual sense – the restless camera movement implies a world beyond the confines of the frame	Static compositions – the limited camera movement implies a stasis in both style and content

Characters and objects are self-sufficient	Characters and objects are controlled by outside forces (i.e. the director)
The director discovers a space	The director creates a space
The audience is a guest	The audience is a victim

Examples of 'open' directors include Max Ophüls, Roberto Rossellini and Jean Renoir; those 'closed' directors include German Expressionists like Fritz Lang and F.W. Murnau, as well as Alfred Hitchcock. The table is a useful methodological framework, for although these distinctions are equivocal rather than absolute (for example, it would be hard to discount Hitchcock's innate understanding of the fluidity and openness of space), the broad formal and stylistic attributes of a particular director means that they can often fit broadly within either category. I would argue that Le Jour se lève – and Carné – can be unequivocally placed into the 'closed' film column. Closed films require clearly defined geometric and architectural homogeneity to fit into the schema, a dependency on a single controlling vision, and mobilize objects and characters into a rigid matrix of spatial configurations. Allan Thiher has suggested that there is a metaphysical aspect running throughout Carné's Poetic Realist films, whereby 'the events that lead to destruction are determined not from within, by some inner causality, but from without, by some transcendental force that ensures that the protagonists never realise their love and liberty'.[3] Another way of defining this 'transcendental force' is 'determinism', something a 'closed' filmmaker appropriates as a means of expressing the stories they wish to tell.

The claustrophobia of Le Jour se lève originates from the fastidious arrangement of space that precludes any sense of movement or fluidity, while its plot architecture – the tripartite ebb and flow into the past and back into the present, and its consistent return to the space of the apartment room – resembles an Escher-like narrative spiral. It is this continuous looping that rigidly pins down the film's protagonists and prevents them from moving out of the spatial configurations designated by Carné. Moreover, the film lacks the multiplicity of viewpoints traditionally afforded in open films. Both the film's characters and its viewers are given controlled access to Le Jour se lève's spatial and narrative configurations through a predetermined – or 'closed' – set of camera positions and editing techniques.

Escher-like narrative spirals: staircase-as-storyline

Structure

In *Poetics*, Aristotle established the 'three unities' as the rules for classical drama. These were the *unity of action* (a play should have one main action that it follows, with no or few subplots); the *unity of place* (a play should cover a single physical space and should not attempt to compress geography, nor should the stage represent more than one place) and the *unity of time* (the action in a play should take place over no more than 24 hours).[4] Much of *Le Jour se lève*'s overall impact resides in the way the narrative corresponds so closely to these structural simplicities laid out by Aristotle. The economy of structure was something that immediately appealed to Carné, as he later wrote: 'I fell in love with it. Not with the plot, which was almost non-existent [...] but with the manner of its construction.'[5] The most noticeable aspect of this construction is the use of three flashbacks which recount the events leading up to François's suicide.

Before the credits for *Le Jour se lève* begin, a title card of white letters on a black screen appears:

Un homme a tué … Enfermé, assiégé dans une chambre, il évoque les circonstances, qui ont fait de lui un meurtrier.

[A murder has been committed … As he sits alone, shut inside a small room, a man tries to reconstruct the events that led to his becoming a murderer.][6]

It is a curious 'opening' to a film, a cumbersome text that ruptures the time-worn conventions of opening sequences. This pre-credit title card did not, however, appear in the film when it was first shown. It was inserted by the film's producer Pierre Frogerais after initial previews of *Le Jour se lève* had proved confusing for the audiences unaccustomed to the technique of flash-backs. *Le Jour se lève* was revolutionary for audiences hitherto accustomed to a strict adherence to simple narrative trajectories and conventional story structure. Yet the flashback structure was no simple selling point or authorial flourish by Carné. Instead, it fulfils a broader strategy, assigning the film its tragic aesthetic and enabling a 'cliché gangster-film situation [to acquire] a complex dramatic structure.'[7] The flashback structure was the deciding factor for Carné, for he implicitly realized that the circular framework would allow the film's mood of fatalism to develop in a rigorous and poetic way. As François lies on his bed besieged by memories, the inevitability of his demise is configured right at the outset. The film's dominant emotional and narrational registers are unwavering: because we have already seen it happen, what will happen must happen.

In cinema, the flashback can be broadly defined as 'an image or a filmic segment that is understood as representing temporal occurrences anterior to those in the images that preceded it';[8] or, in other words, a device that breaks up the narrative's chronological order and allows the story to return to the past and to narrate a particular event within the narrative. The shift in temporality between the two narrative fields can be signalled using a variety of tropes: a voice-over (Joan Fontaine murmuring 'Last night I dreamt I went to Manderley again' in *Rebecca* [1940]); a dissolve (usually accompanied by a visual blurring of the present into the past, familiar to *film noir*); or an intertitle ('Rome. 2000 years ago') are the most common codes. These techniques all appear in *Le Jour se lève* as a means of extensively signalling temporal shifts – the aforementioned title card, the dissolve into and out of the past through the gradual superimposition of one shot upon another, accompanied by the sound of a piccolo on Jaubert's soundtrack, and François's first voice-over recalling and recounting the past ('And yet is seems like only yesterday […] Do you remember?'). As David Bordwell has suggested, flashbacks offer a fascinating instance of the overarching power of objective narration. They are usually motivated as mental subjectivity, since the events we see are triggered by a character's recalling the past. Yet, once we are 'inside' the flashback, events will typically be presented from a wholly objective standpoint.[9]

Bordwell's insistence on the differences between subjectivity and objectivity is important, because flashbacks are ultimately a representation of memory and thus of subjective truth.

Even by 1939, flashbacks were a relatively new cinematic technique. An earlier extensive use of flashback and voice-over narration was found in Preston Sturges's *The Power and the Glory* (1933), in which Ralph Morgan returns from the funeral of his best friend Spencer Tracy and recounts the story of Tracy's life to his wife through a series of elliptical flashbacks. It would not be until 1941, and Orson Welles's *Citizen Kane*, that a more experimental mode of film narration that relayed information and retold stories from singular or multiple perspectives would be introduced.[10] From that point on, flashbacks and voice-over narration became two of the defining tropes of *film noir* and the detective film. They were devices that allowed the past to be reconciled with and integrated into the present, but also, crucially, introduced a sense of doomed inevitability, a *fatum implacum* that hung heavy over the whole of the film. French audiences had already been exposed

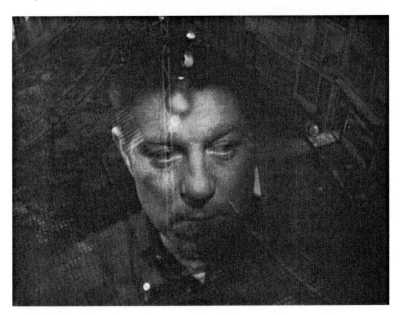

The first flashback: past and present merge

to the flashback in Renoir's *Le Crime de monsieur Lange*. Here, the details of the events leading up to the murder of an unscrupulous businessman and the subsequent fleeing of the murderer are recounted to a group of men. Yet where Renoir's film differs from Carné's was in its sustained retelling of the past – the film is, in effect, one long flashback, bookended by an expository and concluding scene. For Turim, *Le Jour se lève* reverses cause-and-effect order, 'giving us the effect, murder, first, and the cause, and overwhelming psychic tension, following that'.[11] Accordingly, in *Le Jour se lève*, the move into and out of flashback is more persistent, and instead of using a collage of other people's thoughts and statements to explicate a state of mind, the film is solely concentrated on François's individual subjective remembering.

The past-present structure neatly dovetails. There are three flashbacks: the first recounts how François meets and falls in love with Françoise; in the second, François has an affair with Clara; and in the third, François kills Valentin, a man who has had sexual relations with both Françoise and Clara. Enveloped around each of these flashbacks are four sets of events taking place in the present: firstly, the murder of Valentin and arrival of the police; secondly, the arrival of the police fusillade; thirdly, François shouting down to his co-workers assembled in the square; and finally, François's suicide and the release of a tear gas canister in his bedroom.

The following table allows a closer inspection of the film's structural intricacies.

TIMEFRAME	SEQUENCE	SEQUENCE LENGTH
1. Credits		2 minutes
2. Present	François's hotel room	11 minutes
3a. 3 months previously	François's workplace	22 minutes
3b.	Françoise's home	
3c.	*Café-concert*	
4. Present	François's hotel room	6 minutes
5a. 1 month previously	Clara's hotel room	24 minutes
5b.	*Café-concert*	
5c.	Greenhouse	
5d.	Clara's hotel room	
6. Present	François's hotel room	6 minutes
7. Preceding night	François's hotel room/arrival of Valentin	7 minutes
8. Present	François's hotel room	7 minutes

On closer analysis, a number of points become apparent. For instance, this sustained use of particular locations is typical of Carné's insistence upon intricate and claustrophobic sets. The recurring use of repeat spaces – two hotel rooms and two workplaces – also links back to the *Kammerspielfilm* tradition that inspired Carné. It is also clear that time and remembering are important thematic and structural elements of the film. Finally, the film returns again and again to François's room. All the formal aspects of the film – narrative, visual, structural – mark the room as a space of retreat and withdrawal, a spatial unifier to all the other points of isolation in the film. Its closed-circuit, claustrophobic coordinates may restrict movement and hinder meaningful communication – it is telling that we never see François and Françoise together in the room – but it also functions as a womblike space, welcoming, protective and – until the final conflagration – safe. What is also important is that the sequences set in the past last twice as long as those in the present. Approximately 53 minutes of the film's running time is devoted to events in the past, as opposed to around 30 minutes in the present. Such a structure establishes a determinism, a 'concatenation of events'[12] that leads inexorably to the hero's death, and proves that cinema can depict the workings of the mind and not just physical events.

André Bazin once wrote that '[t]here is probably no film in all of cinema more secretly haunted than *Le Jour se lève*, or one where there is less room for chance'.[13] This 'less room for chance'; or, put another way, 'fate', is an important aspect of Poetic Realist cinema. It is expressed both formally (through set design, lighting and music) and structurally. *Le Jour se lève* is just one of a number of French films of the late 1930s which pits a working-class hero struggling to overcome the implacable sense of fate to such an extent that each narrative was – like the nineteenth-century novels of Émile Zola – explorations of destiny and determinism. Told in the first person, François's flashbacks reveal that the present can only be explained by the past. As the film moves mathematically towards its inevitable denouement, this fatalism is sealed with the inevitability of daybreak and a ringing alarm clock: both show an indifference to François's fate and the relentlessness of a universe that is unconcerned with justice or the redemptive power of love.

Set design

Poetic Realism depended heavily on the pictorial for its creation of atmosphere, and this stark visual quality was manifested most explicitly in a stylized and accentuated decor. If any one set can be said to represent the visual and architectural specificities of 1930s French cinema, then it is the apartment block in *Le Jour se lève*. Henri Agel wrote that the set 'sears itself into your mind';[14] it was the film's 'central star',[15] like 'a cliff rising over a landscape of rivers of iron and clouds of soot'.[16] From a position of historical retrospection, argued Michel Perez, it resembled a 'lightning rod created to attract the storms of destiny'.[17]

The apartment block represents what Charles and Mirella Jona Affron call an 'embellishing' design scheme. They define this type of decor as '[v]eri-similitudinous yet unfamiliar and intentionally arresting [...] oblig[ing] the spectator to read design as a specific necessity of the narrative'.[18] These embellishing sets often rely on specifically selected objects or props that discharge symbolic resonances throughout the film narrative to transcend the constructed, framed world and communicate more profound thematic aspects of the narrative. The apartment block is the focal point of the entire film, and indeed can be read as a character in its own right. Trauner's best work with Carné was characterized by liminal sets that enclosed the diegetic world and established a sustained narrative crucible. As well as the apartment block in *Le Jour se lève*, the first appearances of the bridge in *Hôtel du Nord*, the Boulevard du Crime in *Les Enfants du paradis*, the castle in *Les Visiteurs du soir* and the Métro station in *Les Portes de la nuit* each delineate a clear spatial arena that anchors the protagonists and drives the narrative. It is as if these sets are too large for their narratives to contain and are waiting to burst beyond the parameters of the frame and take on a life of their own. They are all examples of what Susan Hayward has termed Trauner's 'hyper-reality' – his sets 'become more significant than the original to which they refer and because of their excess obtain more signification than the narrative which they are intended to illustrate'.[19]

Due to its placement at the confluence of three streets, the apartment block is immediately foregrounded as the key action space for the film, a spectacle not just for the viewer but also for the diegetic community. Its monumentality is heightened by the fact that it is the only tall building in the frame; it is located at a junction, automatically increasing its spatial prominence and, by towering over a largely denuded townscape, it is imbued with a strange, dreamlike presence. Maureen Turim has referred to the capacity of architecture to define the space of cities both physically and metaphorically. She argues that no inscription of architecture produces so dramatic a delineation of the cityscape 'as does the monument whose utility is often limited to the symbolic register and whose frequent placement at

Setting the scene

intersections of urban thoroughfares commands the multiple points of passage and perspective'.[20] What Turim suggests is that monumentality and representation are interlinked; that the symbolic register of a landmark comes to represent not just a certain part of the city but also the very area it overlooks. Consequently, by setting up a contrast between the apartment block and the rest of the surrounding urban environment, the former's prominence is accentuated, and its status as landmark consecrated.

Paraphrasing the narrative

Many of the most successful Poetic Realist sets paraphrase narrative concerns and provide visual shorthand images that eschew the need for lengthy exposition or explication. François Albera writes that several French design schemes of this period 'were not content with simply defining their occupants, but they determined them, and looked to model their behaviour on a spatial structure'.[21] Set design is descriptive; not a silent shell standing detached from the action, but something imbued with a powerful dramaturgical and symbolic charge. Accordingly, decor provides a wider interpretative matrix enabling the spectator to 'read' *Le Jour se lève*.

The settings are highly symbolic. For instance, the apartment block functions as a microcosm of late-1930s French working-class society; the greenhouse functions as an illusory site of freedom where François and Françoise act out their romantic fantasies; the *café-concert* is the domain of Valentin's controlling influences and the town square a site of group solidarity. The bar where François and Valentin meet is another common sociological space in 1930s French cinema, rich in familiar iconography (travel posters, Byrrh advertising, stock characters) with rituals of language and gesture deeply engrained in the national culture. Underpinning these larger spaces are more quotidian fragments immediately identifiable to the spectator. The opening sequence includes cobbled streets, gabled rooftops, a horse and carriage and a Dubonnet sign.[22] By establishing this quintessence of the decor – what Thiher calls 'the sociological average'[23] – and maintaining a balance between established detail and aestheticized reality, Trauner creates a narrativized set. Watching *Le Jour se lève*, one is struck by the perfection of this dialectic, in which we see a familiar urban milieu stippled with poetic flourishes, like the electric pylons, or the metallic tramlines, or the fact that the apartment seems several stories higher than any of the other surroundings buildings. This dialectic between reality and stylization exemplifies Poetic Realist design. This desired fable-like quality – between the real and the accentuated, between the quantifiable and the dreamlike – is the axis on which Trauner's work tilts. His designs for *Le Jour se lève* are exemplary to the degree in which they willingly harmonize at various stages in the film a whole range of architectural registers. In Dilys Powell's memorable phrase, the genius of Carné and Trauner was in their ability to transform 'the tawdriness of the everyday' into formal beauty.[24]

Le Jour se lève also relies upon smaller recurring architectural details to interrogate thematic concerns. Doors, windows and staircases serve both as functional devices and stylistic punctuations. These fragments resonate with powerful literal and figurative significance, indicating how architecture is employed in *Le Jour se lève* to underpin the exigencies of the story. For example, the apartment block's central winding staircase is employed as a means of underlining the occupants' sense of intimacy and togetherness. As the police move up the staircase to interrogate François, Carné's camera shoots down its five flights, complete with inquisitive heads peering out and looking upwards. The staircase now shifts from symbolizing group solidarity towards a sense of suspicion and fear. There are also numerous shots through the stair banisters during this opening sequence, reinforcing the sense of entrapment running throughout the film. This visual motif of imprisonment is further heightened by the shot of the woman walking down the stairs holding a birdcage. Later on, as the first flashback unfolds and François heads off to work, the staircase is reinscribed as a site of community. People call out and greet him, as he walks down the stairs whistling contentedly. François's freedom in this instance sharply contrasts with the immobility afflicting him in his room. Windows, too, are key indicators of entrapment. Like the shot of Gabin and Michèle Morgan gazing out of the window in *Le Quai des brumes*, symbolizing the stasis and the wistfulness inherent in that film's aesthetic mode, François is trapped behind the windows of his apartment, condemned to look out of them at the world below. It is staring out of the window that initiates François's first flashback, and in turn the window will be smashed by gunfire.

Likewise, the multitude of doors is revealing of deeper narrative concerns. Throughout, doors function as architectural editors, regulating comings and goings and marking transitions between two scenes. Doors have an insistent presence in Carné's films and their ubiquity hints at an ever-evolving transition not just from functional objects to poetic markers of passage, but also to an increased understanding of a character's own moral and emotional development. Doors provide or deny knowledge, collapse the space between public and private and function as an elaborate meta-theatrical device. The murder of Valentin is committed behind a closed door, and when the police threaten to storm François's room, he barricades himself in by pushing the wardrobe against the door. When François and Clara are together in her room, Valentin spies them through a hole in the door, marking him out as an unscrupulous eavesdropper who is prepared by stealth to transgress boundaries. Turk has written of Carné's insistence upon the reciprocity of art and life in *Les Enfants du paradis* as predicated upon 'a theatricalised world founded upon seeing and being seen. In such a world, demarcations between the public and the private – doors, screens, drapes – exist only to be obliterated'.[25] This is also apparent in the opening scene of *Le Jour se lève*, where, crucially, we hear but do not see the murder of Valentin. The door at the start of the film will move through a series of transformations – initially, here, as a narrative barrier, a frustrating obstacle that heightens suspense and casts causality into question. Later on, it is a literal obstacle, as the wardrobe is pushed against in to provide an extra barricade against the police gunfire. Doors – like windows – serve as protective entry and exit points for François. Once one becomes walled up and the other rent asunder by bullets, the inevitability of his death is confirmed.

Claustrophobia

The major corollary of Trauner's expressive set design is an overwhelming sense of claustrophobia. In the three bedroom sequences, François is literally caged in his room. The entire *mise-en-scène* works to create this feeling of incarceration – François is wearing striped trousers, and takes a striped tie out of a striped paper bag. The wallpaper and mattress cover are also heavily lined, and a criss-cross lattice chair is clearly visible in the background. This aggregated aesthetic of imprisonment is a constant reminder of the film's visual and symbolic strategy, and conforms to Colin Crisp's observation that several late-1930s films are marked 'by the tragic inability of protagonists [...] to escape from the trap of social reality'.[26]

By placing the wardrobe against the door, François is not barricading himself in temporarily, but walling himself in permanently. This confirms Carné's entreaty to Trauner during pre-production to design a set that is 'completely closed up [...] giving the impression of a man walled up in his room, spending his last night as a condemned man might spend his last night in a cell'.[27] The sense of closure and isolation was made clear by Carné's desired mode of production practice, for, to heighten the sense of restriction, Carné instructed his design team to construct the apartment room so that four interlocking flats could be easily manoeuvred to accommodate the camera and lighting. This decision meant that Carné could film Gabin moving from one side of the room to the other, from the window to the door, from the bed to the mirror, in one shot, without recourse to clumsy edits or obtrusive cuts.[28] The inherent claustrophobia of these spatial schematics was a vital part of the film's overall impact. David Thomson has written how Hitchcock always insisted upon 'sets that fit the other definition of the word – rigid, enclosing, as with traps that are set'.[29] This observation exemplifies Trauner's work on *Le Jour se lève*, wherein decor functions as a trapping device. His sets are like 'traps that are set' because they architecturally and figuratively represent a *huis clos* from which no character can escape. Indeed, it was Trauner who persuaded the producers of *Le Jour se lève* that François needed to be isolated on the fifth floor of the apartment block. The original outline was to have had François living on the first floor, but, as Trauner successfully argued, this would have dissipated all elements of suspense and isolation and would have provided a far less adequate architectural signifier for François's mental state.[30]

Raymond Durgnat once wrote that film architecture can 'constitute an X-ray photograph of the heroes' minds';[31] in other words, the claustrophobic set design in *Le Jour se lève* is analogous to François's state of mind. At several points in the film, decor becomes the clearest embodiment of his struggle, and as the narrative unravels, issues of fracture and identity instability are played out. For instance, in his notes for the screenplay, Prévert wrote:

> Try to make sure that the mirror is not only slightly starred but shivered into several fragments, each giving a slightly distorted angle of reflection, so that in a later scene, François has great difficulty in finding his own reflection when he tries to shoot at it.[32]

The 1930s French studio system, with its insistence upon studio-designed decor, thus provided ideal conditions to isolate and rupture François. Gabin is filmed on several occasions lying on his bed, cigarette in hand, jammed into the corner of his room, between two interlocking walls. Both Carné and Trauner frequently make Gabin the recurrent object of this transferral of emotion from the external world onto the micro-architecture of the set. As we have already noted, Gabin represents on the one hand vulnerability and passivity and on the other a barely concealed eroticized rage. The chiaroscuro lighting and shadowy set design that dominate so many of his films with Duvivier, Grémillon and Carné often express this duality within his living space and his personality. The use of light and shadow in his personal milieu is a potent metaphor for this duality in his personality. The 'look' of Poetic Realism functions as a metaphor for interior rites of passage, in which the Gabin character is imprisoned and his individuality crushed.

In *Le Jour se lève*, the positionality of Gabin within the built environment is highly significant, as he is inextricably locked into his environment through a variety of techniques. In his earlier Poetic Realism films (such as *Pépé le Moko* and *Le Quai des brumes*), gates and walls function as physical barriers regulating his access to and from different spaces. Yet what is telling about the proliferation of enclosed domestic spaces in *Le Jour se lève* is the way in which all of the characters, and not just François, appear isolated. In Clara's room, the tight angles and constrictive spaces reflect the essential world-weariness of her character. There is a picture of Jean-François Millet's *The Angelus* on her wall, which, given that the painting reflects humbleness and spiritual peace, might be read as an extension of her character. The room full of hanging white linen in Françoise's room may embody purity and innocence, but hers is a negatively-charged space. It is cluttered and dimly lit, and the nearby railway line – promising a journey *away* from the centre towards the unknown – offers only an illusory notion of escape similar to one offered by the ship arrivals and departures that François notices in the paper. Postcards from Nice and Monte Carlo adorn Françoise's mirror, but these are, crucially, non-visible places; heard of but not seen. Given his reputation, we cannot even be sure if the sender of the cards, Valentin, has been to these places. Like François, Françoise must cope with these images of fantasy configurations of an elsewhere that will always remain out of reach. As Crisp notes, '[b]ecause the orphan has no "home", no sense of belonging, no community, he or she is vulnerable to victimization by the "criminal" class – namely the rich and powerful.'[33] Both François and Françoise are left in a state of perpetual drift, exacerbated by a set of objects around them which are full of negative associations.

A 'décor phosphorescent': Bazin's experiment

Bazin's seminal 1948 article on the confluence of decor, objects and narrative in Le Jour se lève – 'Le Décor est un acteur' – examined the way in which certain privileged elements of the decor acquired a narrative function. Bazin argued that the decor in Le Jour se lève possessed either a dramatic function or a decorative function ('un décor d'ambience').[34] To corroborate his thesis, Bazin conducted an experiment in the early 1950s. At the end of each screening of the film, he asked audiences to list all the furniture they had seen in François's apartment. Seven pieces of furniture were always remembered – the bed, the table, the mirror, the wicker chair, the armchair, the wardrobe and the night table – and yet the small chest of drawers was recalled by only around a quarter of the spectators. When asked to list the objects in the apartment, similar patterns emerged. Spectators recalled the teddy bear, the broach, the lamp, the ashtray, the cigarettes, the matchbox, the football and the photographs, but not the bicycle parts or a lunch-pack. For Bazin, the conclusion was clear: these non-recalled objects were the only 'to have not, at any moment, had any dramatic function'.[35] Props and furniture that were remembered by the audience had been foregrounded and dramatized in the course of the film – the football was a sign of François's love of sport, the photographs on the wall symbolized a lost past and the wardrobe acted as a barricade against the rest of society.

Bazin's evaluations of the experiment encapsulate several of the key elements of Le Jour se lève:

> We can see how Carné's realism tends towards the poetic transposition of a setting, while remaining meticulously true to life. It does not do this by modifying it in a

formal and pictorial way [...] but by releasing its inherent poetry, by constraining to reveal its secret links with drama. It is in this sense that we can talk of Marcel Carné's 'poetic realism' [...] *Le Jour se lève* is perfect in that its symbolism never takes precedence over its realism, but rather the one complements the other.[36]

Bazin's deconstruction of the *mise-en-scène* marks his study out as a key interpretative text for *Le Jour se lève* and, by extension, for the specificities of French Poetic Realism. The recognition that decor was an amplifier of narrative concerns was an explicit acknowledgement that the depiction of milieu was insufficient to establish a connection between individual and environment. What was necessary was a milieu that visualized the narrative and mirrored individual emotional and mental states.

The furniture, objects and props in François's room were anchored to a recognizable reality that formed 'an astonishing social documentary'.[37] Carné and Trauner achieved optimal saturation, choosing a decor that contributed to the overall meaning of the film without drawing attention away from the underlying narrative imperatives. Only by first structuring and modulating a verisimilitudinous design scheme could decor then function as emotional amplifiers of the narrative. As Bazin concluded, it is 'as if poetry only begins to glow precisely when the action appears to be identified with the most life-like details'.[38]

Style

In his 1929 *Cinémagazine* essay, 'La caméra, personnage du drame' ['The camera as dramatic actor'], Carné praised the German filmmaker F.W. Murnau for his willingness to adapt technological innovation to his own cinematic style. He noted that Murnau's camera opened out and explored the decor, recalling how – in his masterpiece *Sunrise* – the camera 'slid, soared, glided, [and] edged through wherever the narrative demanded [...] becoming a "character in the drama".'[39] Carné reasoned that camera movement was a way of showing off the set and imbuing it with 'to-be-looked-at-ness' that aggressively foregrounded its own narrative importance. Designed to elicit wonder from the spectator by 'displaying themselves', Carné's films frequently contain a series of graceful and complex tracking and panning shots that compels the viewer to read *mise-en-scène* as a particular necessity of Carné's narratives. By taking advantage of the mobile camera to privilege his complex spatial configurations, the tracking shot became one of Carné's most recognizable signature motifs.[40]

Camera movement and framing

The opening sequence of *Le Jour se lève* reflects how far Murnau's stylistic traits had been appropriated. The film begins with a static image of the town square, but the camera quickly frees itself up. A horse and cart trundles into the foreground, and the camera follows, leading the spectator into the diegetic arena and elegantly panning upwards to provide the first sustained image of the apartment block. Through a further combination of pans and tracking shots, the camera then explores the architecture and inner dimensions of the apartment block. This complex sequence – lasting approximately one minute – is interrupted by the sounds of raised voices, a gunshot, a well-dressed man backing out of a door and slumping down a staircase, and then the cries of the blind man: 'What happened? What is it? What's the matter?' This opening scene is a key example of how Carné's elegant deployment of panning and tracking shots 'pierce through to reveal the truth';[41] a fusion of technology and voyeurism that creates narrative tension at the film's outset, and will only be resolved as the flashback structure unravels. Such techniques are exploited several times in *Le Jour se lève*, and anticipated in the opening shot of *Les Enfants du paradis*, in which a long tracking shot, analogous to the spectator's gaze, fleeting and uncertain amidst the teeming panorama of the Boulevard du Crime, introduces the film's spatial parameters. Thus, the camera frames both the monumentality of the decor and the indispensable human figure within that space, privileging them both. As the tracking shot permits this movement within the space most readily, the set can now be 'shown off' and made an object of contemplation. Anne Villelaur recognized this display aspect in *Le Jour se lève*, arguing that 'so many camera movements […] seem to take pleasure in exploiting this photogenic decor'.[42]

Given that the universe Carné often wishes to explore is cramped and claustrophobic, the technical flourishes that epitomize the openings of Carné's films are gradually replaced by more restrained camera movements. Although Crisp argues that this alternation between virtuoso and static camera movements is a relatively common practice in 1930s French cinema, it has important implications for Carné.[43] His sober style seeks – as per the 'closed' film mode – to display a particular state of mind and systematically explore individual moods and motivations. Camera movement thus triggers developments in the narrative. The first flashback is triggered by a steady track towards François's face, and as Carné's camera 'burrows inward',[44] the dominant registers of fate and determinism are progressively unravelled. Such controlled, understated movements help to lay bare the essential details of the

story and the design, and provide an ironic counterpoint to the more sweeping negotiations of space in the opening sequence. When Françoise invites
François into her room and closes the door behind him, we do not cut from
outside her house to inside. Rather, Carné's camera tracks right, alongside
the house, and watches from behind the window as the two embrace. Such
restraint seems suited to the tentative nature of François and Françoise's
burgeoning relationship. Commenting upon his style, Carné later argued:

> I directed my films with a good deal of spareness and rigour; there is never any
> technical ostentation; there is, rather, a certain classical flow [...] To movements
> of the camera, I prefer movements of the heart [...] What interests me is being on
> top of characters, discovering their reactions to certain events.[45]

Framing is also important in establishing the film's sumptuous visual style.
Carné's films frequently employ long shots to establish an individual or group
within the wider diegetic landscape and, as we have seen, the first appearance
of the apartment block in Le Jour se lève is in long shot, signalling its central
narrative role. On other occasions, Carné uses close-ups of faces to capture
an emotional response. This is most evident in the framing of François,
where we see a close-up of his face as he looks out of the window during the
flashback transitions, as he sits on the chair while the police try to shoot him
and as he contemplates suicide. Framing here reinforces François's heightened
psychological state, but also aid the cadences of the film by interspersing
these moments of solitude with more intense dramatic action.

Editing

Using Carné's films from 1936 through to 1950 as a model, Colin Crisp writes
that the edit rate of French classical cinema was characterized by progressively
shorter average shot lengths (ASL).[46] In keeping with the general trend of
a decline in ASL from approximately 15 seconds in the mid-1930s to nine
seconds by 1950s, Carné's films see a similar drop-off: Hôtel du Nord has an
ASL of 13 seconds, while Juliette, ou la clef des songes is nine seconds. Crisp
has noted that that the ASL of Le Jour se lève is 12.5 seconds, which is about
the norm for the late 1930s as editing intensity increased. Of the 420 shots in
the film, over 10 per cent last longer than 45 seconds;[47] indeed, some shots
of François walking around his room last up to 90 seconds.

Such nuances of editing are important. As we have seen, events in the
narrative present are much shorter than those in the past, although the
fluctuations between the two timeframes become less and less invasive as the

film develops. The movements backwards and forwards in time lend events a transcendental feel, for aside from the final gunplay and François's tirade to the crowd, the action throughout *Le Jour se lève* is slow and deliberately paced. It is as if the inner mechanisms of the film mirror François's own realization that events and their consequences are slowly overpowering him. The long takes and static camera set-ups pin down the characters and examine them, and allow Carné to edge ever closer to his scalpel-like examination of the human condition. Bazin noted that the use of dissolves and superimpositions by Carné's regular editor René Le Hénaff has 'a transparent quality [and] the spectators interpret them as only half true, part dream and part reality'.[48] Editing thus destabilizes and condenses time, and the transitions between memory and reality endured by François are felt as acutely by the viewer. Many of the long takes of François in his room serve to draw attention to the passing of time and the relentless move towards a preordained narrative conclusion. Other spatial shifts in the sequences set in the present (such as the transition between the interior shot of the blind man hearing the body fall down the stairs and the exterior shot of the police being led to the apartment block) are announced by a series of left-to-right wipes that substitute one image with another through a sweep across the screen. This more intrusive editing technique, alongside Le Hénaff's less obvious editing, suggests that Carné's wider formal style can oscillate between elegance and expressionism.

Indeed, we can borrow Valerie Orpen's notion of 'expressive editing' to describe Carné and Le Hénaff's editing style. For Orpen, such editing 'is intended to be seen and to be responded to, not just on a denotative, factual level, but on a figurative, connotative level as well'.[49] Two sequences serve to show how editing practices impart information and cue shifts in narrative tone and register, and also reveal the film's undertones. In the sequence shortly after François has shot Valentin, alternate cutting rhythms are used to introduce the film's star actor (Gabin), and place him as the central character in the drama. We hear Gabin before we see him – at the start of the film, before he shoots Valentin, and then, a few minutes later, when the police officers come to question him – and get our first look at him, back to camera, after he has fired his revolver through the door (shot 1). In the next shot (shot 2), Gerbois open his apartment door and the camera pans from him to François's door. François emerges onto the landing and we see him in medium-shot. He looks down the landing, and then across to Gerbois, but there is no cut to Gerbois's reaction. Instead, the camera stays tight on François as he moves to the banisters, and only once he passes Gerbois does his neighbour speak to him. There is another cut (shot 3) to a high-angle

Our first look at Gabin/François

shot of the stairwell (François's point of view [POV]), and then a cut to him in close-up (shot 4), lit from behind and above, his face partly in shadow. There is a medium-shot of Gerbois, who reacts with surprise (shot 5). He has seen the revolver in François's hand (shot 6 is the revolver in close-up) and retreats back to his room (shot 7). François does the same and shuts the door behind him. We then cut back inside François's room (shot 8) and the camera pans and tracks around the room as he picks up the little brooch, removes a tag from his new tie and opens his wardrobe. He then rests against his chest of drawers, puts his hands in his pockets, looks back at the door and waits. These eight shots are a mixture of seamless editing practices (shots 5–7 are the classic shot/reverse-shot technique) that foster logical and non-distracting narrative continuity and more psychologically inflected rhythms (shot 8), in which cutting is nonexistent to better place the main protagonist in their environment and observe them simply going about their business. This final shot of François walking around his room lasts 60 seconds – the entire *plan-séquence* becomes all the more dramatically intense because there is no cut to outside his room, and the emphasis on the passing of time generates tension. Editing here is used very sparingly to suggest François's growing internalized psychological crisis, and is also crucial in withholding Gabin's entrance – we hear him, then see him from behind, then in medium-shot, before the close-up. Such a fragmented presentation of Gabin builds audience anticipation and confirms his star quality.

Later on, as this table shows, when François shouts down from his apartment window to the crowd in the town square below, more rapid editing rhythms are deployed to draw our attention to François's increasingly fractured relationship with those around him:

SHOT	DESCRIPTION OF SHOT	LENGTH
1	François at window of apartment block (long shot)	5 seconds
2	Reverse shot of crowd – François's POV (LS)	3 seconds
3	François at window (medium shot)	1 seconds
4	Man looking up at François (MS)	0.3 seconds
5	Man looking up at François (MS)	0.3 seconds
6	Man looking up at François (MS)	0.3 seconds
7	François at window (MS)	4 seconds
8	Two men looking up at François (MS)	2 seconds
9	Two different men looking up at François (MS)	1 second
10	Blind man and three other men looking up at François (MS)	3 seconds
11	François at window of apartment block (MS)	27 seconds
12	Reverse shot of crowd – François's POV (LS)	1 second
13	François at window (MS)	7 seconds
14	Man looking up at François (CU)	0.3 seconds
15	Woman looking up at François (CU)	0.3 seconds
16	Man looking up at François (CU)	0.3 seconds
17	François at window (MS)	7 seconds
18	Man and woman looking out of hotel window (MS)	0.3 seconds
19	Woman looking out of window (medium close-up)	0.3 seconds
20	Woman looking out of window (medium long shot)	0.3 seconds
21	Apartment block (LS)	1 second
22	François at window (MS)	4 seconds

As Orpen states, 'the essential ingredient in the making of a star is the reaction shots of other characters in the film'.[50] The almost identical shot and editing patterns in shots 4–6, 14–16 and 18–20 reinforce François/Gabin as the focus of both viewer and diegetic audience. The rapid transitions between these shots also reinforce the importance of the interaction between François and the rest of his local community, but also – as the framing moves from close-up to long-shot – the distance developing between them. The reactions of the local community to the unfolding drama are also revealing. They seem generally curious throughout – the blind man persistently asks 'What's happening?', and François tells the crowd 'What are you waiting for?' – and they only become more vocal once Françoise arrives shortly afterwards. This scene is all about Gabin 'performing', complete with the usual *explosion de colère*. Yet, as the editing here reminds us, we are a world away from Gabin's earlier examples of community entertaining. Unlike his singing in *La Belle*

The centre of attention

Équipe and *Pépé le Moko*, which binds disparate communities together into a cohesive, unified whole, the staging of Gabin's performance piece here is characterized by rapid cutting and long-shots, techniques which are emblematic of distance and a highly dramatic register. Far from being unobtrusive, Carné and Le Hénaff's editing choices richly renegotiate Gabin's relationship to his diegetic community.

Lighting

As befits a film profoundly influenced by the compositional textures of German Expressionism, the lighting style in *Le Jour se lève* is, like the set design, highly expressive. German émigré cinematographer Curt Courant created lighting effects that systematically paralleled the architectural mood of the film, complementing Trauner's set designs, and offering a second stylized correlation to the inner angst of the characters. Aggressive shadowing inherited from these Expressionist traditions would be 'projected onto objects and people in such a way as to distort them and defamiliarise them'.[51] As well as the introduction of omnidirectional spotlights to obtain a concentrated lighting source that allows the actors in *Le Jour se lève* to be more precisely differentiated from their backgrounds, the recent developments in panchromatic film created more dramatically defined facial contours and densely layered colours and tones. Courant, alongside Carné's 1930s cinematographers (Eugen Schüfftan [*Drôle de drame*, *Le Quai des brumes*], Roger Hubert [*Jenny*] and Armand Thirard [*Hôtel du Nord*]) modulated these new stylizing techniques, and incorporated window frames and grilles into their lighting schemes so that evocative patterns could be thrown onto walls and faces Although the lighting effects in *Le Jour se lève* are not as forcefully textured as in earlier works such as *Hôtel du Nord* and *Le Quai des brumes*, there is still evidence of Carné's predilection for high-key lighting. Now, Carné, Courant and Trauner evoke feelings of anxiety and hopelessness through carefully modulated lighting palettes and a compatible set design in which 'dead' space is filmed out of focus and audience attention is concentrated on the foreground action. The expressive capacity of light is evident in the opening scene, when Valentin stumbles out of François's room after being shot. Here, the staircase banisters cast long diagonal lines across the walls, introducing a key motif of imprisonment. Shortly afterwards, a low-angle spotlight illuminates the revolver in François's hand.[52] Elsewhere, when the police fire through his window, three repeated shots show Gabin's eyes moving from left to right (as he watches the bullets hit the mirror). This practice of filming Gabin with a ray of light over his eyes offset by darkness in the rest of the frame was initially developed by Julien Duvivier and cinematographer Jules Kruger in *La Bandera*, *La Belle Équipe* and *Pépé le Moko* to introduce 'a softness and vulnerability in [Gabin's] otherwise rugged face'[53] and highlight the actor's star quality, centralizing him diegetically and signalling his status as the film's tragic figure. Such practices are more than just decorative prettification, for throughout *Le Jour se lève*, lighting changes cue the beginning of each flashback, as if the light shining in François's eyes is the sensory catalyst to the very act of remembering. As each flashback begins, there is a close-up of François's eyes and then a slow dissolve into the past events. Consequently, lighting lends a deeper resonance to François's realm, interacting with the decor to apply an evocative textural sheen to both the 'poetic' and the 'realist' aspects of the film.

Sound (and silence)

According to François Porcile, Jaubert's score for *Le Jour se lève*

> represents the most audacious and riskiest attempt: to challenge the dominant descriptive, anecdotic and sentimental conventions of film music and return it to its essential function, that of the expression of time.[54]

Indeed, the film is invested with a rich tapestry of sound, with a variety of sonic and aural layerings infiltrating both past and present sequences. The score functions in the same way as other elements of the *mise-en-scène*: it accompanies, reflects and expresses moods. It also appropriately heightens the tension and underpins the sense of impending fate, most notably in the final few scenes as the police close in on the apartment. The score is typical of much of 1930s French film music, which Michel Chion has described as 'less keen on sweeping strings', and one that privileged 'a solo instrument, such as the saxophone, emerging from the orchestra'.[55] By moving away from Hollywood-style modes of orchestration (woodwind, strings and brass), Jaubert and other French composers (like Joseph Kosma, Vincent Scotto and Georges Auric) evolved a modernist approach to film music. Rather than the formulaic approach that was the common industrial standard in the American context, they developed musical scores that added to the action through a gradual process of accretion, rather than resorting to musical redundancy, tautology or an all too obvious emotional tonality.

As with the richly textured production design, Jaubert was successful in paraphrasing mood and atmosphere, using music as a means of representing

François's kaleidoscopic mental processes. The repetition of the drums is analogous to a heartbeat, its regularity connoting both the passage of time and rising tension. Ambient sound is also carefully balanced with the soundtrack. The sounds of ambulance and police sirens, traffic noise, machinery in the factory and people's voices in the town square all add layers of verisimilitude, grounding the narrative in a recognizable space.

There are 25 musical sequences in the film in which Jaubert uses his score to alert the viewer to the temporal complexities of the narrative, generate passages of transition when the film shifts from past to present and provide clues as to the kind of mood both composer and director are seeking to evoke. For example, the music employed in both the opening and closing sequences is revealing in this respect. At the start, a drum and a low-pitched piano hammer out a rhythmic, repetitive theme. This looping 'obsessive, oppressive'[56] quality introduces the all-pervading sense of inevitability which, like the succession of cigarettes François smokes, underlines the inexorable progression of time.

As the following table shows, Jaubert uses a small range of instruments consistently to introduce and maintain the overall sonic effect.

SEQUENCE	INSTRUMENT	DESCRIPTION	REPETITION
1	Kettle drum, drum, piano	Opening titles	
2	Kettle drum	7:05–8:02 François locks himself in his room	
3	Kettle drum	11:20–11:35 Exterior shot through window of François in room	Repetition of sequence 2
4	Kettle drum, drum	11:35–11:55 François paces up and down his room	Repetition of sequences 2 and 3
5	Kettle drum, drum	12:17–13:29 François evades gunfire and moves to window	Repetition of sequences 2, 3 and 4
6	Piccolo, oboe	13:30–13:46 Transition to first flashback	
7	Brass instrument	14:00–14:20 François's journey to work	

8	Piano, double bass, saxophone, violin	27:21–28:19 Background music at *café-concert*	
9	Piano, double bass, trumpet, violin	28:26–32:16 Background music for Valentin's act	
10	Piano, double bass, trumpet, violin	33:13–35:37 Background music for acrobat act	
11	Piccolo, oboe	35:37–35:53 End of first flashback; transition into present	Repetition of sequence 6
12	Kettle drum, drum, piccolo	35:54–38:09 François turns from window, walks round room, lies on bed, smokes	Repetition of sequences 3 and 4
13	Kettle drum, drum	38:40–39:18 François smokes, police shoot through bedroom door	Repetition of sequences 2, 3, 4, and 12
14	Kettle drum, drum	41:04–41:58 François moves from wardrobe to bed	Repetition of sequences 2, 3, 4, 12 and 13
15	Piccolo, oboe	41:58–42:16 Transition to second flashback	Repetition of sequences 6 and 11
16	Trumpet	53:16–53:43 Man plays trumpet outside café during first François-Valentin confrontation	Repetition of sequence 9
17	Barrel organ	56:09–1:02:27 Love scene between François and Françoise	
18	Piccolo, oboe	1:06:17–1:06:31 End of second flashback; transition into present	Repetition of sequences 6,11, and 15
19	Kettle drum, drum, piccolo	1:06:32–1:06:55 François throws brooch out of window	Repetition of sequences 3, 4, 12 and 13

20	Kettle drum, drum, cymbal	1:07:04–1:08:22 François walks round room, breaks mirror	Repetition of sequences 2, 3, 4 and 5
21	Piccolo, oboe	1:12:18–1:12:23 Transition to third flashback	Repetition of sequences 6,11, 15 and 18
22	Piccolo, oboe	1:19:14–1:19:31 End of third flashback; transition into present	Repetition of sequences 6,11, 15 and 18
23	Kettle drum, drum, piccolo	1:19:32–1:20:22 François lies on bed	Repetition of sequences 3, 4, 12, 13 and 19
24	Kettle drum, drum, piccolo, brass instrument	1:23:08–1:25:08 Police advance; François commits suicide	Repetition of sequences 3, 4, 12, 13, 19 and 23
25	Brass instrument	1:25:50–1:26:19	Repetition of sequence 7

Jaubert's most impressive work is in the two short musical themes that accompany the dissolve into and out of each flashback – the equivalent of those shimmering lines or voice-overs that conventionally introduce the flashback in most films. The first theme (heard six times, in sequences 6, 11, 15, 18, 21 and 22) is a piccolo and oboe, the second a deeper, more percussive rhythmic sound played by a bass drum. The music attains a compulsive, almost tormenting quality, its repetitiveness and trancelike sound becoming highly connotative of François's descent. During events taking place in the past, there is very little diegetic or non-diegetic noise in François's apartment. Indeed, aside from the sounds of bullets, only Jaubert's score penetrates this cocoon (sequences 2–5, 12–14, 19–20, and 23–24). For example, as François paces metronomically across his room, he stops in front of the mirror, lifts a chair and throws it at the mirror, shattering it. As the mirror breaks, the music abruptly stops – it is as if this act of violence has cathartically expunged the pain of François's memories, with the symbol of those memories (the mirror) broken. Yet, after a few moments, the music starts again, low and monotonous, once again invading François's architectural and mental space. By this point, music and memory, past and present, have become interlaced, and the obsessiveness of Jaubert's score works 'to convey the rattle of François's inner voice during the film's passages from objective to subjective reality'.[57]

Jaubert's score is not simply a decorative element 'conveying' moods and cueing appropriate emotional responses for the audience. The music, like the set design, the costume and the lighting, is indicative of the way that the best examples of Poetic Realism sublimated a whole range of cinematic elements into the final film. As André Bazin wrote:

> If one could experiment by running [...] Le Jour se lève solely with the dialogue, and without the music, one would perceive the film as emptied of a part of its sense; the psychology of the characters would be impoverished, the action less clear. The music here does not constitute an accompaniment; it is incorporated into the action; it constitutes in its own way its own action.[58]

The Carné 'touch' – 'his sense of methodic *mise-en-scène* [...] and his almost Neoclassic concern for a film's formal balance'[59] – is exemplified by the successful interaction between narrative structure, set design, editing, framing and lighting in Le Jour se lève. It is a film that corresponds closely to the 'closed' mode of film aesthetics, with its recourse to determinism and its fastidious architectural arrangement that mirrors the narrative's pessimistic register. Yet a visual analysis of the film only partially accounts for the film's consecration as *the* classic example of French Poetic Realism cinema. Le Jour se lève starred three actors who have come to emblematize the acting styles, vocal register and performativity of 1930s French cinema, and the interactions between Gabin, Berry and Arletty mentioned briefly earlier need to be expanded. Moreover, given the circumstances of its filming and the timing of its release, Le Jour se lève demands to be read as an amplifier of contemporary socio-political concerns. In this next chapter we will turn to an analysis of the film's performances and interrogate its political and social dimensions.

Notes

1   Maureen Turim, *Flashbacks in Film: Memory and History* (New York: Routledge, 1989), p. 2.

2   Leo Braudy, *The World in a Frame: What We See in Films* (New York: Anchor Press and Doubleday, 1976), pp. 44–51.

3   Allen Thiher, *The Cinematic Muse: Critical Studies in the History of French Cinema* (Columbia and London: University of Missouri Press, 1979), p. 114.

4   Aristotle, *Poetics* (London: Penguin, 1996).

5   Marcel Carné, *La Vie à belles dents* (Paris: Pierre Belfond, 1989), pp. 140–1.

6   All quotations from the film are taken from English translation of the screenplay: Dina

Brooke and Nicola Hayden, *Le Jour se lève: A Film by Marcel Carné and Jacques Prévert* (New York: Simon and Schuster, 1970).

7   Edward Baron Turk, *Child of Paradise: Marcel Carné and the Golden Age of French Cinema* (Cambridge, MA, and London: Harvard University Press, 1989), p. 152.

8   Turim, *Flashbacks in Film*, p. 1.

9   David Bordwell and Kristin Thompson, *Film Art: An Introduction*, 5th edn (New York: McGraw-Hill, 1997), p. 106.

10 In her article 'Raising Kane' (1971), Pauline Kael argued that *The Power and the Glory* was one of the models for Welles's film.

11 Turim, *Flashbacks in Film*, p. 146.

12 Thiher, *Cinematic Muse*, p. 115.

13 André Bazin, 'The disincarnation of Carné', in Mary Lea Bandy (ed.), *Rediscovering French Film* (New York: The Museum of Modern Art, 1983), p. 134.

14 Cited in Geneviève Guillaume-Griamud, *Le Cinéma du Front Populaire* (Paris: Lherminier, 1986), p. 76.

15 Pierre Billard, *L'Âge classique du cinéma français* (Paris: Flammarion, 1995), p. 336.

16 Georges Altman, '*Le Jour se lève*: une œuvre noire et pure', *La Lumière* (16 June 1939), p. 5.

17 Michel Pérez, *Les Films de Carné* (Paris: Ramsay, 1986), p. 60.

18 Charles Affron and Mirella Jona Affron, *Sets in Motion: Art Direction and Film Narrative* (New Brunswick, NJ: Rutgers University Press, 1995), pp. 82–3.

19 Susan Hayward, 'Luc Besson', in Yvonne Tasker (ed.), *Fifty Contemporary Filmmakers* (London: Routledge, 2002), p. 57.

20 Maureen Turim, 'The displacement of architecture in avant-garde films', *Iris* 12 (1991), p. 32.

21 François Albera, *Albatros: Des russes à Paris 1919–1929* (Milan: Mazzotta and Cinémathèque française, 1995), p. 49.

22 The construction of the town square was paid for by Dubonnet, eager to see their advertising posters displayed so prominently on the side of the apartment block.

23 Thiher, *Cinematic Muse*, p. 121.

24 Dilys Powell, 'Film directors – a talk for the BBC's Third Programme, October 1946', repr. in Christopher Cook (ed.), *The Dilys Powell Film Reader* (Manchester: Carcanet, 1991), p. 40.

25 Turk, *Child of Paradise*, p. 303.

26 Colin Crisp, *Genre, Myth, and Convention in the French Cinema, 1929–1939* (Bloomington: Indiana University Press, 2002), p. 98.

27 Carné, *La Vie à belles dents*, p. 107.

28 Gabin in particular objected to such fastidiousness. 'Tell me when you've finished with your dumb ideas', is how Carné remembers it in *La Vie à belles dents*, p. 107.

29 David Thomson, 'The art of the art director', *American Film* 2/4 (1977), p. 18.

30 When the film was remade in Hollywood in 1947 as *The Long Night*, set designer Eugène Lourié constructed an apartment block in which the François character (played by Henry Fonda) lived on the first floor. Trauner attributed the failure of the film to this architectural decision, which did not correspond to the narrative trajectory or Fonda's psychological state. See Ciment and Jordan: 'Entretien avec Alexandre Trauner (1)', pp. 14–16.

31 Raymond Durgnat, *Films and Feelings* (London: Faber and Faber, 1967), p. 102.

32 Jacques Prévert, '*Le Jour se lève*', *L'Avant-scène cinéma* 53 (October 1965), p. 14.

33 Crisp, *Genre, Myth, and Convention in the French Cinema*, p. 87.

34 Originally published in 1948 under the title 'Fiche du *Jour se lève*' in the periodical *Doc*, Bazin's article is the amalgamation of several presentations of the film he gave to ciné-clubs and post-war symposia.

35 André Bazin, '*Le Jour se lève*', repr. in *Le Cinéma français*, p. 88.

36 Ibid., pp. 91–2.

37 Ibid., p. 93.

38 Ibid., p. 101.
39 Marcel Carné, 'La caméra, personnage du drame', *Cinémagazine* (12 July 1929), repr. in Rober Chazal, *Marcel Carné* (Paris: Seghers, 1965), p. 88.
40 The technique had also been used by Feyder in *La Kermesse héroïque*, the film on which Carné acted as creative assistant.
41 Vincent Amiel, 'Un réalisme raisonné', *Positif* 550 (December 2006), p. 91.
42 Anne Villelaur, '*Le Jour se lève*', *Dossiers du cinéma, Collection Rondel* 4* SW 8271 (Paris: Bibliothèque de l'Arsenal), p. 117.
43 Colin Crisp, *The Classic French Cinema 1930–1960* (Bloomington: Indiana University Press, 1993), p. 394.
44 Turk, *Child of Paradise*, p. 157.
45 Hélène Climent-Oms, 'Carné parle', *Cahiers de la cinémathèque* 5 (Winter 1972), pp. 44–5.
46 Crisp, *Classic French Cinema*, p. 400.
47 See Colin Crisp, 'The rediscovery of editing in French cinema, 1930–1945', *Histoire et Mesure* 2/3 (1987), p. 205.
48 Bazin, '*Le Jour se lève*', p. 80. Le Hénaff had already edited several of René Clair's early films, and he would go on to direct a number of films in the 1940s (e.g. *Le colonel Chabert* [1943] and *Scandale* [1948]).
49 Valerie Orpen, *Film Editing: The Art of the Expressive* (London: Wallflower, 2003), p. 117
50 Ibid., p. 88.
51 Crisp, *Classic French Cinema*, p. 377.
52 A similar effect occurs in *La Bête humaine*, when the sliver of light that slices through the train carriage windows imitates Roubaud's blade streaking down the corridor towards the camera during the Grandmorin murder scene.
53 Ginette Vincendeau, *Pépé le Moko* (London: BFI, 1998), p. 20.
54 François Porcile, '*Le Jour se lève*: une partition de Maurice Jaubert', <http://www.forumdesimages.net/fr/alacarte/htm/ETUDE/LEJOURSELEVE/content.htm> (accessed 8 November 2006).
55 Michael Chion, *La Musique au cinéma* (Paris: Fayard, 1995), p. 131.
56 Porcile, '*Le Jour se lève*: une partition de Maurice Jaubert'.
57 Turk, *Child of Paradise*, p. 153.
58 Bazin, '*Le Jour se lève*', p. 82.
59 Turk, *Child of Paradise*, p. 41.

3   Performance and Politics

Gabin […] is always the pure self, uncorrupted by culture, relying only on the force of his integrity and his singleness of purpose. In a world of compromises he must be doomed, spectacularly doomed.[1]

Defeat struck France as lightning strikes a tree. […] The world, hanging upon the event, was stupefied. […] In every respect the 1930s had undermined the cohesion of French society, recreating old cleavages and complicating them further with new confrontations.[2]

This chapter will examine how key scenes in *Le Jour se lève* – at the *café-concert*, in the greenhouse, the final scene, and others – synthesize the film's thematic, structural and aesthetic preoccupations we have previously outlined. In her influential reading, Maureen Turim offers three possible ways we might read the film: 'as an expression of the mood of despair after the collapse of the Popular Front on the eve of the Second World War', 'as the migration into French culture of Nietzschean philosophy' and 'as Carné's and Prévert's personal fascination with and reworking of the US gangster film of the 1930s'.[3] These 'symbolic' approaches are instructive, and shed light on the film's formal properties, as well as providing useful prisms for exploring Carné's style and tone. What I am particularly interested in is examining the film's performative aspects, for by looking closely at the interactions, networks and patterns of the four main characters, a number of perspectives (performance style, gender, class, socio-political, 'reflectionist') emerge.

Performance styles

We noted in Chapter 1 the importance of Jean Gabin not just to *Le Jour se lève*, but also to the development of French Poetic Realist cinema. Throughout the film, Gabin is constantly at the centre of the narrative, framed or spotlit to accentuate both his sexual and physical potency and his helplessness, and on numerous occasions, the camera positions him as the object of desire for women and the object of identification for men. The Gabin myth of 'charismatic ordinariness',[4] first sketched in Duvivier's *La Bandera* (1935), and gradually articulated throughout the second half of the 1930s, climaxed with the role of François. His very name – François – possesses clear allegorical implications. Gabin 'stands' not just for an individual, or even as part of the whole French working class in *Le Jour se lève*, but, explicitly, for France herself. In 1935, a *Ciné-Miroir* article noted that Gabin

> likes to assume the air of a freethinker, he speaks slang, he shrugs his shoulders, he's simple, frank and open […] and when the occasion calls for it, he knows how to send trouble-makers unceremoniously about their business.[5]

As we shall see in this chapter, Gabin's relationships to and interactions with *Le Jour se lève*'s three other main actors, Jules Berry, Arletty and Jacqueline Laurent, all deploy these types of behaviour. All three actors 'play off' Gabin, and reveal something about François as much as themselves.

Valentin is the charmingly monstrous opposite of François, the harbinger of chaos and disorder, and an embodiment of the political and social forces that threaten François and the class he represents. Jules Berry's performance in the role is fundamental in heightening *Le Jour se lève*'s tragic overtones. He 'attracts by way of compulsion'[6] because his 'otherness' is both disconcerting and beguiling. He is well-spoken and well-dressed, and, crucially, transcends class hierarchies to seduce both Clara and Françoise, whereas François's seductive allure remains class-bound. Berry was born Jules Paufichet in Poitiers in 1883, and was trained as a stage actor, performing in numerous vaudevilles and light comedies before his move into the film world in Marcel L'Herbier's *L'Argent* (1928). From this point on, he was remarkably prolific, appearing in nearly a hundred films between 1933 and his death in 1951. Like Gabin, Berry worked at crafting a particular film persona that resonated across genres and styles. His theatrical flamboyance and dandyish reputation were frequently incorporated into roles that embodied elegance, linguistic dexterity, and no small degree of manipulative condescension. One of Berry's earlier film performances clearly anticipates Valentin – his devious Batala in

Renoir's *Le Crime de monsieur Lange* combined a silver-tongued slipperiness and unscrupulousness that typifies the trickster character honed to perfection in *Le Jour se lève*. Berry is a ghostly presence in both films. Batala fakes his own death, only to return to the publishers (now run by a cooperative) in the dead of night to be killed again; while the audience see Valentin shot at the start of the film, only to reappear several times throughout the film and be killed a second time as the narrative folds back on itself. At one point, he even tells François and Clara, 'It's funny. I reappear like an apparition.' In both films, Berry's slicked-back black hair and waxy pallor hint at a malevolence that would be eventually clinched by Carné in *Les Visiteurs du soir*, where he cast Berry as the Devil. In this medieval allegory, made at the height of German involvement in France, Berry's gestures of 'spontaneity, versatility, and elasticity'[7] were read by some critics as an allegorical portrayal of Hitler.

In opposition to Gabin's naturalistic, authentic and 'ordinary' idiom, Berry adopts a more stylized and declamatory performance mode throughout *Le Jour se lève*. His expressive voice and repeated gesticulations run contrary to Gabin's more internalized acting style, which sets up a clear oppositional structure between the two men. Valentin is demonstrative, a gesticulator prone to grand theatrical gestures and excessive body language. He spies on François and Clara while they are lying on her bed, seeking to share in the kinds of intimate sexual or emotional encounters that are always denied him. His mock-inquisitiveness on being discovered, when François opens the door, is a classic defence mechanism, masking his inadequacy in the face of the dominant heteronormative pairing of François and Clara. Indeed, wherever he goes, he appears as an interloper, out of place in the *café-concert* and the *bar-tabac*, both arenas traditionally populated by working-class characters. His mannerisms, his speech, his costume and his body language all mark him out as 'not-Gabin'. He is an actor forever acting; the malevolent flip side to the genial Frédéric Lemaître, the self-aggrandizing ham actor in *Les Enfants du paradis*. For Valentin, the purity of acting is in the end result, revealing the fundamental hypocrisy at the heart of performance. Like Batala, whose interests are dictated by unstinting greed, *donjuanism* and the continual manipulation of his employees' good will, Valentin exploits the full range of emotional gestures – pity, anger, sincerity – to evoke unwarranted sympathy. When Clara describes him as a 'conjuror' who 'with all that smooth talk, you'd almost think he pulled it out of his sleeve', she makes clear the opaqueness at the heart of Valentin's persona.

If we look at the scene in the *bar-tabac*, when Valentin tells François that he is Françoise's father, we can see Valentin's mythomania at play in three stages. In stage one – what we might term 'revelation' – François listens to the older man's story. The camera tracks slowly around the back of François and frames Valentin in close-up. He begins with his hands clasped, in control, telling François that he has 'tolerated' his relationship with Clara, and is 'broad-minded' enough to let it continue. The choice of words here is important, setting in motion the stream of emotional blackmail and *faux* generosity that Valentin expertly marshals. We cut back and forth between the two, but this is Valentin's show – he becomes more and more solemn, speaking in a low voice, drawing in his audience (both François and us). The big revelation is made more significant by the majestic pause Berry leaves between 'that young girl [...] is my daughter' coupled with the cut to François's dumb-founded reaction in close-up. All the way through this scene, characters and decor in the background of the *bar-tabac* have been filmed in soft-focus; they are spectral presences engaged in an inaudible hubbub. What counts here is the interplay between François and Valentin, and the latter's power play and the beginning of the seeds of deceit sown. Accordingly, the environment shifts from a 'realistic' rendition of a typical social space to something far more oneiric. The dreamlike tone of this exchange is accentuated by Valentin's insistent responses and the abrupt arrival of the patron with the previously ordered drinks, which replaces the shot/reverse-shot pattern with side-on framing.

Valentin 'acting up'

Stage two of Valentin's tactics is 'self-loathing'. This self-pity is signalled by a new posture – hands unclasped, placed contritely across the arms, or stroking the chin contemplatively – and a facial gesture that involves him wrinkling his forehead and avoiding François's gaze. There is only one reaction shot of François in this section – Valentin's performance requires his attention and ours – but when it comes, the reverse-angle shot of him is revealing. Gabin's downturned mouth and resigned look suggest sympathy, even pity. François is himself an orphan, brought up in *assistance*, and so this conversation becomes, through framing and editing, a quasi-reunion between father and son. Prévert's screenplay adds a delicious subtextual layer here – Valentin describes the eyes of Françoise's 'mother' as 'the same eyes, greyish green [...] a colour that changes like the sea in winter'. Like François's 'sad eye and happy eye', eyes here suggest duality and difference, but also, unwittingly on Valentin's part, suggest a union between François and Françoise that we know cannot be sustained.

The final stage – 'authority' – culminates when Valentin brandishes his paternal authority, telling François that he does not think Françoise will be happy with him. Valentin's use of the French subjunctive form here – 'je ne pense pas qu'elle puisse être heureuse avec vous' – is a refined linguistic mark of difference that separates the two men (François responds with a contracted 'T'es formidable' ['Well, if that isn't magnificent'], itself a specific linguistic trait). The editing, so underplayed in the earlier sections, becomes more rapid, as the cuts between the differing reactions of the two men inject pace and momentum into the scene. Now it is François's turn to seize the initiative, grabbing Valentin by the lapels and declaring his love forcefully to his surrogate father/father-in-law-to-be. François leaves, and the final two shots are of Valentin – from behind, nervously tapping his fingers against the bar table, and then in medium close-up, biting his fingernails. David Thomson writes that '[s]tars sometimes just wait, reflect and dwell on themselves in close-ups. Character actors never get that time: they have to be busy'.[8] Berry's busyness is epitomized in this scene which, at six and a half minutes, is one of the longest in the film. His energy, his non-stop talking and his ability to shift emotions all reinforce Valentin's malign, implacable presence. It is telling that the blind man who was the first to discover Valentin's body at the start of the film is also in the *bar-tabac* at the start of this scene – fate, death and Valentin go hand in hand.

The two female performances are also important in establishing the film's tonal qualities and, through their interaction with their male counterparts, have revealing implications for class and sexual politics. Arletty was born

Léonie Bathiat in 1898 in Courbevoie, on the outskirts of Paris, and during the 1920s became a prominent music-hall and cabaret star, famous for her richly sardonic and high-pitched voice. She worked with Carné five times (right up to *L'Air de Paris* in 1954) and has been described as 'the most beautiful woman in Carné's films, the only one who is really a woman'.[9] Her first notable performance was as the prostitute Raymonde in *Hôtel du Nord* (1938), where her memorable exchanges with Louis Jouvet remain some of the most quoted in French cinema and highlight Arletty's trademark *gouaille* (sharp-tongued humour) and raucous insolence. The roles which she played best for Carné were a combination of the vampish and the proletarian, usually complex characters with a tough outer shell that concealed an inner vulnerability. One review of *Le Jour se lève* praised Arletty's ability to exert power over men because she could 'suggest a self beyond their reach, however easy the immediate gift of her body'.[10] This quality of elusive sexuality is evinced in her later work on *Les Visteurs du soir* and *Les Enfants du paradis*, films which amplify and modulate her pre-war performances. In the first, Carné plays on Arletty's gender ambiguity by disguising her as a young page boy, and as Garance in *Les Enfants du paradis*, Arletty employs a cool distancing irony and a *femme fatale* haughtiness that is at odds with her broader 'tart-with-a-heart' register in *Le Jour se lève*.

In her first and only major film role as Françoise, Jacqueline Laurent is the least recognizable of the film's four main stars. She had already featured in René Clair's *Les Deux timides* (1928), and was the French ambassador's daughter with whom Mickey Rooney fell hopelessly in love in *Judge Hardy's Children* (1938). Only 18 when filming began for *Le Jour se lève*, Laurent exerts pureness and innocence that are sharply contrasted by the sordidness, virility and sexual *franc-parler* of the other three characters. Susan Hayward suggests that there are recurring female characterizations in 1930s French cinema: the 'unattainable' (Michèle Morgan, Mireille Balin), the 'animal' (Ginette Leclerc, Simone Simon), the 'foreign' (Annabella, Line Noro) and the 'hooker' (Arletty).[11] Laurent resists these dominant representational paradigms and falls into a new bracket – ingénue. Although some critics found fault with Laurent's performance (describing her as 'weak', 'bland' or 'pallid'), others praised her 'quiet possessive passion' and her 'lovely – perhaps too lovely aggravation'. For *Variety*, Laurent had 'something of the *coquette* about her' but beneath the 'veneer of sentimentality and sweetness lay a mass of conflicting emotions' that an actress as inexperienced as Laurent was unable to carry off.[12] Certainly, her role as passive ingénue is critical in setting up the generic patterns of melodrama that recur in the film. Moreover,

Françoise's profession as florist is replete with dense contextual significance, as it brings connotations of fertility and fragility that ultimately underpin the film's fraught gender relations.

Sequence analysis I: the *café-concert* (26m. 56s.)

The scene at the *café-concert* (named 'La Fauvette' in Prévert's screenplay), in which we see Valentin's performing-dog show, is a concise cameo of the important relationships in the film. It is the first and only time that the four main characters are in the same place together, and their behaviour reveals much about their individual personalities and motivations. The scene is rich in foreshadowing, whereby small, 'invisible' gestures are replayed or recontextualized later on: Françoise fiddles with her compact mirror, Clara mentions the word 'mimosas' and François tells Valentin what he does to people with bad manners. Carné's mathematic narrative precision – his 'closed' style – expertly lays down narrative clues that will have repercussions later on. In a wider sense, the scene also frames notions of the popular and the community and provides a glimpse of the sort of leisure activities the urban working class would have participated in during the 1930s. The

A community is entertained

café-concert became popular in France during the Second Empire (1852–70) as customers paid to hear popular songs, romantic ballads and political and satirical revues. Even though the popularity of the *café-concert* had begun to diminish by the 1930s, as more commercially driven entertainment formats like the music hall, with its greater emphasis on glitz and glamour, appealed to wider audiences, the *café-concert* remained an important leisure pursuit, with its socially cohesive and escapist framework and its corroboration of the new-found representation of the working class in popular art forms. The *café-concert* was thus a cosy communal site of intimacy which 'foregrounds closeness between entertainer and entertained'.[13]

The scene begins with a woman onstage, singing lustily and loudly. She is played by Germaine Lix, herself a singer, who, along with contemporary *chanteuses* like Fréhel, Florelle, Yvette Guilbert and Marie Dubas, served as 'a "woman of the people" who could "evoke the good old days"'.[14] This is a lovingly recreated space, with Lix performing against a painted backcloth similar to the theatrical decor Trauner and Carné would later recycle in *Les Enfants du paradis*. To strengthen this space's social importance, Carné cuts to a long-shot of the stage from the back of the *café-concert*. This communal gesture allows further architectural details to emerge, such as the wrought-iron ceiling beams, the multiple lamps and the tables and chairs full of people. Françoise enters and takes her seat amongst an audience of men, women and children. On stage, François then enters, and the camera follows him as he pays for his ticket and moves to the bar, a familiar central space in the films of the period. All the paraphernalia of the bar space is reproduced by Trauner – zinc counter, bottles, bar tender, advertising – to reinforce its enduring appeal. The camera then adopts François's point of view as he looks at Françoise seated a few rows from the front of the stage. She adjusts her make-up using the compact mirror that we see later on, and the music starts up again to announce Valentin's entrance. *Mise-en-scène* is again important: the entire dog show is framed proscenium-arch style, fixing Valentin as the centre of attention, and during the act, there are a series of shot/reverse-shots which alternate the point of view of both diegetic and non-diegetic audience. This reinforces the status of the *café-concert* as a site of popular spectacle, for longer takes throughout the act strengthen this bond between performer and spectator. As we have seen, Valentin is adept at crowd-pleasing gestures, and the entire sequence is a sustained meta-theatrical performance that he himself is constantly 'directing'. He flings his arms wide, removes his top hat and white gloves, and introduces his assistant, Clara, whose own short black tutu and sequined bodice are deliberately provocative. He is comfortable on stage, leading the dogs through an elaborate routine and teasing the audience with conspiratorial sideways glances typical of showmen. Clara then subverts Valentin's control by deliberately letting his hat fall to the ground and walking offstage in the middle of the act. We are initially unsure whether this behaviour is all part of Valentin's act – the archetypal 'straight man' repartee – but once we see his angry reaction (momentarily unmasking his stage-persona poise and hinting at well-concealed unscrupulousness), we understand that this is someone who exerts a powerful controlling influence on those around him – dogs, assistants, audiences.

All the while, François looks on, silently. There are three near-identical shots of him leaning at the bar, out of sight of Françoise, carefully observing the action. Clara emerges from backstage, and the camera tracks alongside her as she threads her way through the audience to the bar. Her first words to François are a frank description of Valentin – 'la vache' (the bastard). They begin talking and turn their backs to the stage, blocking out Valentin's performance. As Clara talks to François at the bar, she is encoded as sexually predatory – the coat she wore to cover herself as she walked to the bar is now discarded, and she asks François to buy her a drink. She describes Valentin's storytelling abilities:

> He can tell you all sorts of tales, and you fall for them. I mean take the Côte d'Azur, for instance […] He's only got to talk about it and there you are. You're in it, up to the neck. That's how I fell for him […] mimosas.

On hearing 'mimosas', François repeats the word and turns around abruptly, to look at Françoise. This is an example of Gabin's deliberate use of movement as a way of conveying a shift in behaviour or thinking. Throughout this whole scene, he has been still and observant, but the mimosas trigger a memory. Clara, on the other hand, never stops talking; she's the one making the effort to establish some romantic connection with François. She tells him that she always takes off her make-up before going to bed, and says 'You've got blue eyes. They're nice and calm and restful' (for Vincendeau, Gabin's blue eyes suggest 'romantic love and "otherness"'[15]). The *mise-en-scène* alters substantially, with Carné deploying a set of tight medium close-ups between the two actors to establish intimacy. Light sparkles off her bodice, thus heightening her desirability, while the general hubbub of the *café-concert* is progressively muted, so that their exchanges become more prominent. To clinch the deal in what seems like remarkably quick time, Clara concludes: 'I've had enough of men who are always talking about love. It's true. They talk so much about love that they forget to make it.' His response – 'I'm not always so absent-minded' – coupled with a sly, knowing look foreshadows their romantic liaison. This sexually charged banter – similar to later famous exchanges between Humphrey Bogart and Lauren Bacall in *The Big Sleep* (1946) – is interrupted by the return of Jaubert's music and a long shot of the stage, complete with a troupe of bicycling acrobats. After sending Françoise home leave the *café-concert*, Valentin returns to the bar to confront Clara. He assumes a much more sinister presence, far removed from the slightly ridiculous stage persona he had only recently adopted. Now, clad in black fedora and ermine-lined greatcoat, he seeks to re-establish control over Clara and reassert his authority. He grabs her, but François intervenes, moving between the two of them.

This nine-minute scene is expertly choreographed by Carné, who frames the various interactions between the four protagonists against the backdrop of the *café-concert* community. The acts presented at La Fauvette collapse the boundaries between popular and bourgeois. This is reflected in their staging – rather than the segregating aesthetic of the later music halls and cabarets which 'seduced at a distance',[16] these spectacles initiate common bonds between populism and the popular. Even Valentin, that most classic bourgeois 'type', positively revels in his 'low culture' status of dog trainer. It is revealing that the final stage performance of a group of acrobats cycling round and round in a circle is followed by a dissolve back into the narrative present. François now wanders back and forth in his apartment, reading a newspaper and muttering aloud: 'Ship movements. Ships arriving at Boulogne, on the 6th, the *Veendam*, coming from New York on the 13th, *Noordam*, coming from New York. Ship movements.' It is as if Carné and Prévert are reminding us that the cycling acrobats – like François – are futilely 'going nowhere', but are at least doing it with a smile. Gabin as François seeks escape, perhaps again by boat, as he had hoped for at the end of *Pépé le Moko* and *Le Quai des brumes*. Yet audiences attuned to the 'Gabin myth' in his 1930s films recognize that breaking free from one's surroundings is impossible, and that the only attainable freedom is death.

Gender politics

The quadrangle of desire between François, Valentin, Françoise and Clara is laden with revealing sexual, psychoanalytical and melodramatic overtones. *Le Jour se lève* reverberates with the generic and textual aspects of the male-centred melodrama common in 1930s French cinema and conforms to a persistent metanarrative, which, according to Ginette Vincendeau, 'privileges a strong, often eroticized, relationship between a mature man and a young woman'.[17] What makes *Le Jour se lève* particularly significant is the manner in which the interactions between the four are consistently destabilized. The brooch in particular becomes a device that links past and present timeframes, and means different things to the four main characters. In the first flashback, it has a denotative value – Françoise pricks her finger while she tries to put it on. In the second flashback it assumes a greater narrative significance, for Françoise gives it to François as a sign of her affection. Still in the second flashback, its meaning is destabilized when Clara informs François that the brooch was given to Françoise by Valentin as a prize for having slept with him. In the narrative present, François throws the brooch out of the window in a defiantly symbolic gesture, no longer believing in the redemptive power of her love. The use of the brooch to control our alignment with person to person emphasizes power relations and generates audience sympathy, creating a 'psychoanalytic narrative economy'.[18]

On the surface, Arletty and Laurent provide alternate depictions of femininity in *Le Jour se lève* that mirror the differences between Gabin's aggressive masculinity and Berry's campness. As we saw at the *café-concert*,

Three sides of a love quadrangle: Valentin, François and Clara meet

Clara is mischievous, acerbic, teasing. When François visits her apartment, she has clearly just emerged from the shower. François's rather puzzling reference to her as 'Truth rising from the well' – 'truth' here connoting nudity, and a proverb that Prévert would use again, for Arletty, in *Les Enfants du paradis* – is clarified when one recalls that this scene was censored. A famous still photograph exists showing Arletty's naked body, her nipples clearly visible, smiling as she emerges from the shower. Françoise is codified as the opposite of Clara, and for many spectators François's infatuation with Françoise (over Clara, his more obvious match) is the major narrative weakness of the film. While it is true that in certain scenes – for instance, when she learns of François's fate – her performance is unconvincing; it is also the case that she, more than any other character, should clearly be read symbolically. The scene when Françoise and François meet for the first time introduces these allegorical implications. They share a name day, both were brought up in orphanages, and she first appears as the pure embodiment of innocence, wearing a white dress and carrying a bunch of azaleas. Yet the symbolic connotations of purity, innocence and a shared past are unsustainable once the azaleas wither in the factory. As Allen Thiher states, the introduction of the *femme-fleur* (that 'woman-flower' representing the apotheosis of the Surrealist love ideal) is 'part of the world of illusory, hothouse flowers that

Françoise, the *femme-fleur*

cannot exist outside this world of artifice'.[19] The mutual compatibility hinted at in the first meeting between François and Françoise is quickly engulfed by the fatalism of the film.

Yet despite their apparent rigid generic and characterization patterns, Clara and Françoise are somewhat unstable female archetypes, overlapping rather than diverging. For one thing, Clara's playful demeanour and brazenness represent an attempt to mask her own feelings of regret that emerge at several points in the film. She often talks ruefully to François – 'Luckily we don't love each other' – and when Françoise, delirious in grief at the end, says, 'He doesn't love Clara, it's not his fault', Clara's subsequent tears reveal a character 'brought face to face with a wasteful life and the ageing process'.[20] Françoise is also far worldlier than she first appears. The idealized version of Françoise, established earlier in the factory, is skewed when she excuses herself from spending the evening with François to visit Valentin at the *café-concert*. There's even some emotional gameplaying going on, when she asks François, 'You're not going to be jealous, are you?' Later on, as she leaves the *café-concert*, she tells Valentin that he has spoilt her evening by not spending time with her. There is a double implication here – is she disappointed because she cannot sleep with Valentin, or because she has rejected the opportunity to sleep with François (whom she has not noticed at the *café-concert*)?

If we look at two scenes in which François is alone with Clara and Françoise, we can see the film's ambiguous exploration of gender and sexual politics. When François and Clara lie on her bed together, they initially appear as 'one of the rare healthy and minimally neurotic couples in Carné's works'.[21] There's a barely concealed sexual attraction (this time instigated by François in a reversal of Clara's earlier *café-concert* 'chase') that is reinforced by Carné's framing, with Clara in close-up, gazing up at François as he talks. When he says that wants 'a little bit of shade', Clara moves to the window to draw the curtains, but sees Valentin arrive. Thus the illusion of safe domesticity and sexual intimacy remains exactly that: an illusion. Not only does Valentin's arrival (and subsequent eavesdropping) destabilize the harmony, but because François ultimately remains fixated by the pureness of Françoise, Clara will, from this moment on, be de-sexualized, transformed from enticing seductress emerging from the shower to the weeping maternal figure at Françoise's bedside, caring for the young ingénue.

When François visits Françoise in her room on the edge of town they have already been together for three weeks. They talk together in the kitchen in low voices, ostensibly because her employers are asleep in the next room. Yet Prévert's screenplay notes deliberately call for 'muffled whispers' and 'an almost intangible silence' throughout their exchanges, as if to invest this entire conversation with an extra layer of romanticism. White linen and sheets hang from rafters to create a comforting *espace blanc* into which François can comfortably regress, away from the noise and pollution of the factory. With iron in hand, Françoise is now equated with a laundress, another mythic role in 1930s cinema that represents a 'form of absolution for the worker's daily implication in industrial sin'.[22] Françoise then goes to change into a darker dress and the camera adopts François's POV, framing the door as he waits for her to emerge. His reaction, in medium close-up, is a bashful lowering of the eyes, and his question – 'Did you make yourself beautiful just for me?' – is ironic, given that we realize in the next scene that she has got ready to see Valentin, and most probably wanted to spend the night with him. François's relationship with Françoise thus remains frustratingly chaste: his last two gestures in the scene are to suck her finger after she has pricked herself on the brooch pin and to take the teddy bear with him as a surrogate trophy. Françoise's relationship to François remains both aligned and opaque. A patterning between them is established through the decor of her bedroom, complete with its central mirror and bed under the window, but then her decision to leave and see Valentin rather than stay with Françoise destroys this ideal image of the ingénue set up in the previous scene in the factory.

Valentin's role in this quadrangle is to bring about its destruction. Noël Burch and Geneviève Sellier have highlighted how a number of 1930s films tangentially address the issues of incest in the form of a triangular relationship in which a powerful father figure displaces a younger man/suitor for the affections of a younger woman.[23] This incestuous-couple paradigm is directly played out in *Le Jour se lève* from the moment Valentin tells François that Françoise is his 'daughter'. It sets in motion François's Oedipal trajectory and his attempt to negotiate this patriarchal crisis. When François shoots Valentin, it is a manifestation of purgative violence of the most sustained kind. The catalyst for François's shooting of Valentin is the former's preoccupation with Françoise's virginity and the latter's ability to invoke feelings of jealousy and sexual inadequacy. Their final confrontation begins with François sitting on his bed, winding up his alarm clock, only half listening to Valentin's paranoid ramblings. Valentin craves control, telling François, 'You've got to tell me exactly what's going on with Françoise', and justifying the lie that he is Françoise's father: 'I am a man of imagination, a dreamer. I invent things to amuse myself.' François becomes increasingly exasperated by Valentin's constant movement – 'Stop moving around like that. You remind me of a rat [...] Keep still, I tell you, Keep still!' François tells Valentin to stop talking three times in this scene – as he pushes him to the window, after he picks up the brooch and then after Valentin's final speech:

> As for me, they don't love me ... but they want me ... And that's everything: to be wanted! And since she wanted me, if you see what I mean ... the child and I ... I would have been wrong to restrain myself ... I love youth ... Are you interested?

It is this verbalizing of the defilement of the 'daughter' that is the catalyst for François to shoot Valentin. François's choice of words corroborates this reading. Before firing, he shouts 'tu vas *la* taire' ('will you not reveal it/not say it') instead of the expected 'tu vas *te* taire' ('will you keep quiet'), i.e. it is the very revealing/saying of Françoise's loss of virginity that causes the murderous impulse. Sexual jealousy does for François in the end, but he is pushed towards murder inexorably by Valentin. Maureen Turim has written of François's death-drive throughout *Le Jour se lève*,[24] but Valentin is as much a part of this death-wish patterning, for it is he who brings the revolver to the apartment and throws in onto the table, within François's reach: he comes to the apartment both to die and to 'kill' François, a notion supported by Carné's deft *mise-en-scène*. Towards the end of their confrontation, the two men face off against each other, both shot from over the shoulder. On the table, the revolver is prominently displayed, within François's grasp. Valentin continues the goading, until he is shot. Their final exchange – 'See where it got you now... And you?' – reveals Valentin's motivations all along. Gabin's murder of the incestuous paternal figure is not as sustained as his killing of Michel Simon in *Le Quai des brumes* (instead of striking him once with the stone, Jean adds three more blows), but both killings are frenzied. Yet the paroxysm in *Le Quai des brumes* is directed towards a villain clearly depicted as paedophilic and degenerative; Valentin's 'otherness', on the contrary, is more amorphous. He is an amalgam of the weak 'father' and the malicious individual whose motives remain inexplicable, the showman *raté* who manufactures tawdry pleasure by branding his dogs with hot irons. The commercial success of *Le Jour se lève* (and *Le Quai des brumes*) can in part be attributed to the solace offered by explosive and purgative violence against the abject 'father'.

Sequence analysis II: the greenhouse (56m. 14s.)

The six-minute greenhouse scene is perhaps the most romantic in Carné's entire oeuvre. It begins with a fixed camera, framing François and Françoise in a two-shot medium close-up with flowers and plants all around them as she tells him that Valentin is not her father. François's language – 'he makes me sick', 'the most despicable rat' – is at odds with the exotic setting, even more so as it is underscored by Jaubert's lush soundscape. Françoise sits down on a mound of straw matting and again the camera keeps a respectful distance, as if the tenderness of the developing love scene is too fragile for close inspection. After the tracking and cutting of the previous scene between Valentin and François, Carné uses a more restrained *mise-en-scène*, only switching to a sustained close-up of François (complete with subtle lighting on his face, immaculately coiffed hair and cloth cap) once he recounts his history of bad luck. Françoise's role throughout this monologue is to stay silent and return his gaze, although her glistening lips and pale face, coupled with her flowery dress, continue to bolster her role as François's object of desire. Her gaze is also one of empathy, of understanding, and not just one of restless physical yearning. There is a sense for the first time in their relationship that this is an exchange of equals, for both have renounced their other lovers. François then delivers the quintessential Gabin/Prévert speech:

> You know when you're waiting for a tram and it's pouring with rain – the tram doesn't stop … Ding! Full up. So you wait for the next one … Ding, ding! Full up, full up. The trams all go by … Ding! And you stay there, you wait … But now you're with me, everything's going to be different.

This is not the cool, detached love scene that Carné's critics felt it to be (Gérard Guillot regarded Carné's direction here 'as cold as the panes of glass on the greenhouse'[25]). Instead, the sequence is suffused with a bittersweet melancholy and a stoic resignation, and the sentiments voiced here by François – undaunted optimism, romantic faith, the hopelessness-anticipation dichotomy – exemplify not only this film's worldview, but the entire stylistic tenor of Poetic Realism. In the final exchange between them, he asks 'Tu m'aimes?' ['Do you love me?']. Her reply – 'Oui […] je t'aime' ['Yes […] I love you'] – is the first time that she uses the less formal *tutoiement* register when talking to François. Their love is now mutual, equal, and, as if to confirm this reciprocity, Jaubert's rising strings and woodwind signal a moment of excess and provide a deeply ironic counterpoint to the developing fatalism exerting itself within the present-day timeframe. This 'hypersentimental'[26] scene is similar to the funfair kiss between Jean and Nelly in *Le Quai des brumes* – both play out declarations of love that provide respite to increasing diegetic tension, both are romantic musical insertions seeking to break through a monotone visual scheme, and both take place against backdrops

Love in the afternoon: Françoise and François in the greenhouse

of artifice (the funfair) and intangibility (greenhouse) that are paradigmatic spatial presentations of Carné's dual concern with reality and stylization.

Prévert's decision to set the love scene here may have been influenced by the 'serre chaude' in Zola's *La Curée*, where the balmy atmosphere exerts the same effect on Renée and Maxime as it does on the plants when their semi-incestuous relationship is consummated. Similarly, some of Belgian symbolist poet Maurice Maeterlinck's most accomplished work is found in *Serres chaudes*; here the soul is claustrophobically imprisoned inside a symbolic hothouse full of animals and plants. Gazing through the opaque glass, Maeterlinck equates the decadence inside the greenhouse with his own moral corruption. In *Le Jour se lève*, this space is full of flowers but they are flowers trapped under glass. The greenhouse can offer only the illusion of real landscape, and accordingly becomes a metaphor for the temporary illusory happiness experienced by both François and Françoise. This scene 'underscores how the decor separates the couple and the outer world'[27] at precisely that moment when they are indulging in romantic fantasies. Both the flowers and the lovers are trapped in the confines of the greenhouse like butterflies trapped under glass. Any notions of freedom or permanence are offset by the artificiality of the surroundings.

Class struggles

Early studies of Popular Front cinema tend to downplay the emergence of the working class, arguing that for all the post-1936 euphoria, the fate of the worker as reflected on-screen did not demonstrably improve. Broadly speaking, these studies argue that the *ouvrier* remained politically and socially marginalized, and that the influence of Popular Front consciousness on 1930s cinema was as limited and short-lived as the Front itself. Georges Altman's famous observation (written in 1931) that the worker in French cinema 'opens doors [...] carries the baggage [...] says "Mme. is served" [...] says thank you for the tip, [and] shouts "Vive la France" in the newsreels'[28] was frequently invoked to suggest that by 1939, this reductive view of the working man had scarcely changed. The worker's ongoing political impotence was also reiterated: the worker-run cooperative in *Le Crime de monsieur Lange* and the *guingette* in *La Belle Équipe* are both framed as utopian endeavours held together by fragile class ties and unsustainable shared visions that quickly fracture under malignant external influences (namely, the bourgeois and the predatory female).

More recently, the situation of the working class in the 1930s has been more positively evaluated, and 1930s French cinema has been repositioned as a 'cinema that celebrated the working man'.[29] This refutes François Garçon's observation that only nine films made between 1936 and 1939 dealt with predominantly proletarian themes and characters.[30] Garçon was only taking into account overtly serious political narratives, ignoring this period's numerous comedies (such as *Prince Boubole* [1938], *Un de la Canebière* [1938], *Fric-Frac* [1939]) which focused on working-class types and tropes. This emergence of a working-class 'iconography and gesturality'[31] – accent, song, social behaviour, architecture – sought to elide the socio-cultural differences between the working class and the bourgeoisie and challenged the ways in which working-class audiences saw themselves. They were no longer viewed *in relation to* the bourgeoisie – as suggested by Altman – but as separate entities closely tied to their own distinct set of topographies and cultural practices. Such a shift had important ideological as well as representational ramifications, since the emergence of a hitherto marginalized class in the wake of 1936 required a cinema that could combine populist aesthetics with underlying social comment to celebrate and ennoble the working class (a cinema that Carné, firstly as a journalist at *Cinémagazine* and then as director of *Hôtel du Nord*, did much to instigate). As Crisp notes, the worker was now commonly presented on-screen as 'vital, dynamic, affectionate, considerate, and with a limitless but unrealised potential'.[32] This 'unrealised potential' in *Le Jour se lève* is epitomized by the François-Clara pairing partially developed during the *café-concert* scene – the promise of a future together (as Clara says, in a moment of honesty, 'It's not every day, you know, that a woman who suddenly finds herself free like this, meets a man she likes [...]').

What was undeniable was that by the late 1930s the Poetic Realist protagonist had become progressively isolated within their urban environment and alienated from their class contemporaries. This trajectory is frequently read as 'the depressing story of fragile ideals fighting the machinery of class politics and modern industrialization',[33] and suggests that this marginalization of the working class partially accounts for the subdued visual tropes of Poetic Realism. Time and again in the late 1930s, the workplace is codified as a place of danger, a place of 'suicidal ennui from which the hero strove madly to release himself'.[34] The sandblasting factory, like the *guingette* in *La Belle Équipe*, the print room in *Gueule d'amour*, the service station in *Le Dernier Tournant* and the trinket shop in *Le Quai des brumes*, are all debilitating workplaces. Gabin excelled at playing tragic working-class heroes, and Bazin's phrase resonates because Gabin's worker identities in the 1930s attempted to transcend the class divisions that the Popular Front government were also hoping to collapse. His powerlessness in the face of forces 'too powerful to allow his continued existence'[35] aligns him with that recurring doomed figure of late 1930s French cinema who was resigned to feelings of hopelessness and stalemate. Indeed, as soon as we see a riderless horse accompany the horse and cart with its rider in the film's opening shot, one thing is clear: François is doomed. It is revealing that in Gabin's nine films from 1935 to 1939, there are seven suicides and eight murders – it is as if the self-destructive tendencies inherent in these films are amplified by the growing political crisis within France. That Gabin's character in *Le Jour se lève* is called François ('France') behoves an allegorical interpretation of his fate, and the fate of the country.

Alongside the gloomy poetry of *Le Jour se lève* reside highly revealing class discourses. The film paints an unrelenting negative picture of working-class life from the moment François cycles to work through a pastoral countryside dominated by huge chimney stacks, electricity pylons and the sound of a factory siren. After a slow dissolve to the factory interior, Carné's camera tracks alongside four workers, each cocooned in the same surreal futuristic rubber suits and helmets, sandblasting large pieces of metal amid deafening noise, before coming to a stop at François. The relentless mundanity of this work is underlined by Carné's avoidance of editing here. The tracking

François trapped by work: sand and sadness

shot past the workers lasts for 25 seconds, and the medium-shot of François at work a further 17 seconds. These men are absolutely defined by their work. François remark to Françoise when she enters the factory – 'It's work, and work is freedom […] and health' – is highly ironic, for this is a dehumanizing workplace, the effects of which are highly deleterious to the health (workers must drink milk to keep their lungs lubricated and counter the sand in their lungs). Françoise's flowers shrivel up seconds after she enters, and the deafening thrum of the machinery impedes communication. François later tells Françoise: 'Oh, and I've had some jobs! Never the same, but it always came to same thing. Decorating, grinding paint, or the lead mines […] that's not much fun either, red lead.' Unlike Clair, who used the automatism of factory life in À nous la liberté (1931) to comically satirize imported business theories of modernization and Taylorism into French factories, or Renoir, whose depictions of workers in Toni (1934) and La Vie est à nous (1936) were inflected with class consciousness and engaged political commitment, Carné does not overtly politicize Le Jour se lève. But this attention to social contexts equate to a sustained cri du cœur that laments the position of a proletariat once again marginalized and exploited, despite the heady future promised in May 1936.

   Further class imbalances are epitomized by the struggle between François and Valentin. Carné and Prévert's political intentions are reflected in the film's representation of the bourgeoisie, as represented by Valentin's vainglorious, adulterous and scheming qualities. For instance, costume reveals oppositional tensions: François stands for the recognizable image of the French *ouvrier*, dressed in conventional proletarian outfit, while Valentin's bourgeois status is assured by the tailored suits he wears and the cape and top hat he dons for the *café-concert*, which underpin his overtly theatrical manner and domineering, ostentatious presence. Even the two men ordering a drink exposes particular nuances: François drinks a *p'tit blanc* (glass of house white wine), Valentin a *fine à l'eau* (brandy and water). As Turk reminds us, such details in *Le Jour se lève* reveal an implicit political context: François's battle with Valentin for ownership of Françoise 'acts out a power play that French society was actually experiencing: the bourgeoisie's attempt to restrain the encroachment on their property by the proletariat'.[36] As we have already seen, this battle for ownership is first articulated at the *café-concert*, where François and Valentin meet for the first time, and each of their subsequent encounters is characterized by class tussle, with one trying to gain power or control over the other. While François uses brute force to assert himself (grabbing Valentin by the collar, threatening to push him out of the window), Valentin's power-play tactics are much more insidious. For instance, he tells François: 'Odd. I always thought workmen had no nerves', and pronounces the words 'un métier manuel' in a way that drips with sarcasm. He thinks nothing of exploiting the degenerative nature of François's job to drive a wedge between him and Françoise: 'Think it over … You've no prospects … no future (*He pauses*) … and no health.' Later on, François equates the hazards of his job with his shooting of Valentin, telling the crowd: 'I'm a murderer […] Everyone kills a little bit, but gently, so you don't notice, it's like sand. The sand gets inside you.' Class struggles are thus mobilized as a means to highlight the ongoing plight of the worker. Whereas Valentin's work is predicated upon artifice and the controlled training of dogs, François's relationship with his work and his fellow co-workers underlines this class-bound reading of *Le Jour se lève*.

In the case of François, the film charts a gradual erosion of positively framed working-class discourses. At the outset, associations with sport encode François as virile and healthy. There is a football in his room, as well as bicycle parts, and we also see him cycling to work and to visit Françoise. These connections with sport and leisure place an emphasis on Gabin's 'physical prowess […] exuberance, and vitality'[37] which help authenticate François's place within his immediate diegetic community. When he walks down the stairs of his apartment block to work during the second flashback,

François whistles cheerfully and greets Gerbois on the staircase. He is tightly bound to this apartment community – the crane shot that follows him lasts 30 seconds – and when the concierge's wife asks after him at the bottom of the staircase, he replies 'Not so bad. And if they get worse, we'll have to manage, won't we', repeating the same response Gerbois gave to him a few seconds earlier. Beneath François's virility lies a stoicism. In the factory, François jokes to Françoise – 'he'll drink milk when cows eat grapes' – as Gaston swigs from a bottle of red wine (a Prévertian flourish, presumably). This is the only time in the film that we see François laugh naturally, and it is telling that it happens at work, with fellow workers.

Such bonds of solidarity become complicated once François rejects the calls of his community. Like the supportive communities in other Gabin films of the 1930s, the workers who gather beneath his window in the town square are 'both central and peripheral, both active and passive [...] passive in the sense that they are not themselves performing, and active through their gaze at, and therefore construction of, the performer, Jean Gabin'.[38] The crucial difference in Le Jour se lève is that while the community *is* active (staring up at François, imploring him to surrender) and *is* passive (silent participants during his angry tirade), there is no restorative reunion or cohesive reassembling of class bonds. By the end, even his fellow

François sustained by work: milk and mateship

workers have been rejected or silenced. It is now François's turn to be the performer, 'entertaining' the crowd from an elevated vantage point. But this is not entertainment of the Valentin style, full of dogs and inflatable balls. François is acting out a personal and a collective crisis for both diegetic and non-diegetic spectator. Whereas the internal shell of the apartment had earlier been coded as a locus of community, the gap between François at the top of the apartment block and the workers at the bottom becomes a divisional space that separates François from his class-bound community. As discussed in Chapter 2, Carné's use of multiple long-shots in this scene shows François alone in his immediate environment, devoid of class ties, with all traces of class awareness eliminated. The rapid repetition of close-ups and reverse shots as he shouts down to them reinforces the spatial and emotional distance between François and the rest of the working class, transforming the urban space into a battleground in which traditional sites of community have been dismantled. By now, the individual as well as the community has been splintered, to the point where François frantically denies his identity:

PAULO: François! Come down! There's still hope.
FRANÇOIS: François? Who's that? François? Don't know him [...] never heard of him! It's over. There isn't a François anymore. Go away, all of you. Leave me alone. Leave me alone.

The town square is now a site of fragmentation, where cohesive social bonds articulated by the poignant cries of the workers – 'François, we will help you [...] There's still hope' – are brutally interrupted by riot police and tear gas. François has oscillated between two contradictory impulses throughout the film. He is the epitome of the Popular Front worker, vital and virile, robustly defined by his work and symbiotically linked to those around him; yet by this point he is isolated, detached from the protective and inclusive camaraderie that the Popular Front sought to foster, waiting to be destroyed. He may rage against the dying of the light but is ultimately a doomed figure, succumbing to a pre-ordained fate common to many of his on-screen alter egos in the late 1930s.

For Turk, this impasse represents 'the ultimate destiny of the average upstanding Frenchman vis-à-vis society, government, and economy hostile to his well-being'.[39] This partly explains why the reception discourses that greeted Le Jour se lève and other Poetic Realist films oscillated so wildly. On the left, critics admired the film for its direct engagement with the manners and motivations of the working class, complete with their frustrations and undermined aspirations. The right-wing press in particular viewed the ideological inflections of these films as dangerous and deplorable. Ultimately, the class struggles at the heart of *Le Jour se lève* replay in miniature a whole raft of debates taking place in France in the aftermath of the Popular Front.

Sequence analysis III: François's death (1h. 19m. 23s.)

The film's final sequence begins with a dissolve, marking a slow transition from the past-tense previous scene, in which François has just shot Valentin. The scene brings us back to the start of the film, closing the narrative circle and fulfilling the promise of the initial intertitle – 'a man tries to reconstruct the events that led to his becoming a murderer'. As in previous dissolves into and out of the past, Jaubert's score lends the early parts of this climactic sequence a melancholic and wistful feel. We have also heard this music before whenever François and Françoise have been together, and so Jaubert's score possesses ironic implications, given the events that will shortly take place. In a reverse shot, we see François sitting motionless on the bed. His sense of resignation is strengthened by his stillness, his cigarette burning slowly in the corner of his mouth and his hands in his pockets. François attempts to light a cigarette but cannot, and throws the last cigarette on the floor. This gesture reminds us of earlier scenes, in which cigarettes have served as a symbol of time – when one runs out, François lights another quickly – but now, as the film draws to a close, François's time is effectively up. At 40 seconds long, it is one of the longest shots in the film, and one of the simplest. It shows Gabin just 'being Gabin' – still, stoic, the epitome of caged masculinity.

There is an abrupt cut to the street outside, jolting us from Jaubert's score and making us aware of life outside. A police van arrives and drives past a long line of police wearing identical clothes and adopting a similar posture. We pan upwards to Clara's apartment, where she tends to the delirious Françoise. Clara is lit from above, which accentuates her faded beauty and sense of goodness. Françoise is feverish and deeply troubled, and the soft-focus lens emphasizes the ephemeral beauty of both characters. Tossing and turning on the bed, Françoise gives an abridged version of the romantic entanglements of the film – 'You see, François, we love each other, but it really doesn't have anything to do with us', 'It's not Clara he loves', 'One can't love everybody at the same time'. Visibly upset, Clara lets out a sob. She moves to her window and looks across the square towards François's apartment, mirroring the earlier scene where Clara and François stared out of her apartment window together. In that scene, she told François:

'I've been happy because of you, really happy, and I'd have liked it to go on […] Only I lived here, and you […] you lived over there. We were too far apart.' Clara's true feelings for François, hidden beneath her brash exterior, are finally expressed in this gesture. This is the last shot we see of Arletty in *Le Jour se lève*, and she would only appear again in a Carné film three years later, in *Les Visiteurs du soir*.

An elegant crane shot moves us from the roof of the apartment (where two police officers are manoeuvring themselves into a position to throw the tear gas canisters) and through the window into François's room. The shot allows Carné to build tension – the viewer, the assembled crowd below and Clara, all know that the police are planning to use tear gas, but François does not. Jaubert's insistent soft percussive drumbeat throughout these final moments maintains the pressure. We cut back into the room and see François still in the same position as earlier – slumped against the wall, trying to keep awake, looking like he has aged 20 years. He looks up, and we see what he sees: bicycle parts, fragments of the broken mirror and the revolver. As the score becomes increasingly fraught (mixing the drumbeat with the François–Françoise tune), François places his hand on his heart. He then looks back at the revolver, and this time it is framed in close-up. An air of inevitability now emerges, especially given audience's prior knowledge of Gabin's usual fate in these sorts of films.

As François moves the mirror and contemplates the revolver, Françoise's ghostly voice-over emerges on the soundtrack – 'You remember what you said? At Easter we'll pick lilac'. Rather than jolting François out of his death-drive, these words seem to serve as the catalyst for suicide. In a scene written by Prévert but (perhaps wisely) abandoned by Carné, Françoise's words were followed by a shot of François and Françoise cycling alongside each other in the countryside, with bunches of lilac on the handlebars. The voice-over is sufficient to remind us that the film trades in Prévert's highly romanticized register, using the simple act of picking lilac at Easter as an unattainable pleasure. Even more so, the words (rather than the images) cruelly recapitulate the myriad motifs of thwarted escape that pervade Poetic Realist narratives.

We again cut to the police officer on the roof and then to the crowd outside, staring up at the apartment in long-shot. Whereas earlier, François's immediate community had been vocal, shot in close-up and urging him to give himself up, it is now silent, distant and non-interventionist. Fate is the only force at work now – social solidarity or the redemptive love of Françoise and Clara cannot help. Back in the apartment, François places his fingers to his heart and lifts the revolver to his chest. It is a slow, methodical gesture, typical of an actor defined by understatement. His death occurs off-screen, for just before the gunshot rings out, Carné cuts to a shot of the police officer throwing the canister through the open window of the apartment. We see François prone on the floor and, as the gas rises, the alarm clock begins to ring and Carné's camera slowly tracks back, displaying the carnage of the room and allowing us to contemplate the various items that have come to define François. After 30 seconds, the ringing stops, and the sense of operatic magnitude in this final sequence is clinched by the crescendo of Jaubert's score, the fade to black and the end-title card.

Although I disagree with Turk's claim that the gradual tracking back suggests a 'symbolic anticipation of France's acceptance of defeat in World War II',[40] it is an unsettling conclusion, made even more unbearable by the ringing alarm clock and Jaubert's mournful score. It is tempting, of course, to search for allusions to Nazism throughout *Le Jour se lève*, given Carné and Prévert's leftist political inclinations (Prévert had once played Hitler in a satirical sketch performed by the Groupe Octobre in 1933) and the attendant political climate. A few scenes contain only implicit inferences – Clara has earlier described Valentin as a man who 'can tell you all sorts of tales, and you fall for them', and when the riot police arrive at they wear

Daybreak: the fragments of a former life

iron helmets and long black overcoats and carry rifles. In a scene cut from the final sequence these parallels are made more obvious when an inspector refers to the riot police as 'bloodthirsty brutes' prepared to kill a hero 'alone against the world'. The removal of these lines thankfully divests the film of overtly cumbersome political allegories without diminishing the underlying current of despondency and despair that the film taps into. Yet 'not mentioning the war' by no means downgrades the film's allegorical heft. As Robin Bates notes, it was the 'sight of such powerful and aggressive males as Hitler, Franco, and Mussolini heading neighbouring governments [that] was deeply unsettling and caused the French to question their own leaders and their capability for action'.[41] The figure of François is an apt symbol for this dysfunctional crisis, not least because he too is cut off, isolated and defenceless at various points in the film.

Nineteen-thirties French cinema is bookended by two very different depictions of urban, working-class existence: *Sous les toits de Paris* and *Le Jour se lève*. Both films play out against stylized studio-designed backdrops, but both offer contrasting depictions of the working class – Clair's film sees class bonds refined and reiterated through community solidarity and collective popular song; for Carné, by the end of the decade, the *populo-prolo* lies barricaded in an airless tomb, surrounded by broken fragments of a former existence, awaiting the impending conflagration. Indeed, it has become somewhat of a standing joke among French film enthusiasts that Jean Gabin would generally commit suicide or be killed at the end of film after film in the 1930s. Jeancolas sees these repetitions as a direct reflection of the times: 'France was suffering from a depression and had to face an increasingly threatening reality: the spectre of war. She didn't want to confront it. She exorcized it with a sacrifice – she sacrificed Jean Gabin.'[42] Such comments about the 'meaning' of *Le Jour se lève* lead us to a more tendentious area: whether or not the film reflects the zeitgeist. Before we look more closely at the reception of the film, we shall examine this issue.

A reflectionist film?

The idea that the films 'reflect' particular political contexts has been around since Siegfried Kracauer's *From Caligari to Hitler* (1947) and has since guided much social film history. Kracauer argued that the cinema of the 1920s Weimar Republic (films like *The Cabinet of Doctor Caligari* [1920], *Nosferatu* [1922] and *Dr Mabuse the Gambler* [1922]) offered a unique insight into the collective mindset of post-World War I Germany, and that by dint of their collective conception and mass consumption, such films reflected society more accurately than other art forms and offered insights into the mindset of their audience. Kracauer's conclusions that 'what films reflect are not so much explicit credos as psychological dispositions – those deep layers of mentality which extend more or less below the dimension of consciousness'[43] represent the classic reflectionist paradigm. Accordingly, reflected readings of *Le Jour se lève* assume that the film evokes the mood of the times – the end of the Popular Front, Munich, the *drôle de guerre*, the Fall of France – and provides an interpretative matrix for the state of the nation in late 1939. By May 1940, Paris was an occupied city; ten months earlier, François, the 'French-man' trapped in his apartment, anticipated the *huis clos*. His sacrificial death offered spectators 'a spectacle of commiseration'[44] amidst the fractures and fissures of late 1930s French society. *Le Jour se lève* encapsulates the undermining of the Popular Front (François) and its usurpation by a combination of empty rhetoric, political grandstanding and the sweeping across Europe of aggressively nationalist tendencies (Valentin).

Such responses, whilst convenient, are highly problematic, not least because they require nuancing. Referring to French Poetic Realist films, Susan Hayward refutes this earlier naive explanationism, 'since not all the films in this grouping necessarily gave this straightforward early-optimism, later-pessimism message'.[45] Indeed, comedies continued to dominant production right up to 1939 (around 50 per cent of studio output). Poetic Realist cinema was part of a much wider terrain of film genres in the second half of the 1930s, and many of the most popular films of this period were highly incompatible with the 'dark' subject manner and gloomy visuals of *Le Jour se lève* and *Le Quai des brumes*. Just as Kracauer's approach can be criticized because of his narrow focus on a set of Expressionist films that was not representative of audience tastes, so too must we remember that Poetic Realist films add up to no more than between 80 and 100 out of nearly 1,000. *Le Jour se lève* was filmed and released at the same time as a number of other films, few of which could claim to 'reflect' the state of the nation in 1939 any more or less than Carné's film.

So while it is true that the best mid-1930s French films 'shared a pessimism attributable to their times',[46] it is more persuasive to see *Le Jour se lève* not as work capturing the zeitgeist or 'responding to' contemporaneous political events, but instead as a plural text made by many different people with different agendas, preoccupations and backgrounds. These proximate, intersecting factors (cultural climate, émigré sensibility, infrastructural changes) make a far more compelling case for a causal connection between 'film' and 'society', between *Le Jour se lève* and the collective anxieties of late-1930s France. Audiences in June 1939 could not have failed to draw parallels between François's status as an immobilized victim of forces beyond his control and their own government's inability to respond to changing political and social turbulence. As Andrew notes, it was the viewers themselves, emerging blinking into the sunlight, who were the ones 'who must live on in the day that has so mercilessly dawned'.[47] And so, it is now time to turn to the reception of the film, to examine the highly politicized responses that greeted the film on its release, and to chart its – and Carné's – rocky afterlife.

Notes

1   Dudley Andrew, 'Poetic Realism', in Mary Lea Bandy (ed.), *Rediscovering French Film* (New York: Museum of Modern Art, 1983), p. 117.

2   Philippe Burrin, *France under the Germans: Collaboration and Compromise*, trans. Janet Lloyd (New York: New Press, 1996), pp. 32–3.

3   Maureen Turim, 'Poetic idealism as psychoanalytical and ideological operation: Marcel Carné's *Le Jour se lève*', in Susan Hayward and Ginette Vincendeau (eds), *French Film: Texts and Contexts*, 2nd edn (London: Routledge, 2000), p. 63.

4   Ginette Vincendeau, *Stars and Stardom in French Cinema* (London and New York: Continuum, 2000), p. 69.

5   Cited in Colin Crisp, *Genre, Myth, and Convention in the French Cinema, 1929–1939* (Bloomington: Indiana University Press, 2002), p. 274.

6   Susan Hayward, *French National Cinema*, 2nd edn (London: Routledge, 2005), p. 173.

7   Edward Baron Turk, *Child of Paradise: Marcel Carné and the Golden Age of French Cinema* (Cambridge, MA, and London: Harvard University Press, 1989), p. 202.

8   Cited in Valerie Orpen, *Film Editing: The Art of the Expressive* (London: Wallflower, 2003), p. 105.

9   Jacques Siclier, *La Femme fatale dans le cinéma français* (Paris: Cerf, 1957), p. 50.

10   Roger Manvell, '*The Long Night* and *Le Jour se lève*', *Sight & Sound* 16/63 (Autumn 1947), pp. 115–16.

11   Hayward, *French National Cinema*, p. 176.

12   Anon., '*Le Jour se lève*', *Variety* (26 July 1940), p. 503.

13   Ginette Vincendeau, 'From the *bal populaire* to the casino: class and leisure in French films of the 1930s', *Nottingham French Studies* 31/2 (1992), p. 61.

14   Kelley Conway, *Chanteuse in the City: The Realist Singer in French Film* (Berkeley: University of California Press, 2004), p. 21.

15   Vincendeau, *Stars and Stardom in French Cinema*, p. 73.

16   Dudley Andrew and Steven Ungar, *Popular Front Paris and the Poetics of Culture* (Cambridge, MA, and London: Harvard University Press, 2005), p. 201.

17   Ginette Vincendeau, 'Daddy's girl: oedipal narratives in 1930s French films', *Iris* 5/1 (1988), p. 73.

18   Maureen Turim, *Flashbacks in Film: Memory and History* (New York: Routledge, 1989), p. 147.

19   Allen Thiher, *The Cinematic Muse: Critical Studies in the History of French Cinema* (Columbia and London: University of Missouri Press, 1979), p. 123.

20 Keith Reader, '"Mon cul est intersexuel?"': Arletty's performance of gender', in Alex Hughes and James S. Williams (eds), *Gender and French Cinema* (Oxford and New York: Berg, 2001), p. 70.

21 Turk, *Child of Paradise*, p. 173.

22 Crisp, *Genre, Myth, and Convention in the French Cinema*, p. 93.

23 Noël Burch and Geneviève Sellier, *La Drôle de guerre des sexes du cinéma français 1930–1956* (Paris: Nathan, 1996), p. 14.

24 Turim, 'Poetic idealism as psychoanalytical and ideological operation', pp. 63–77.

25 Gérard Guillot, *Les Prévert* (Paris: Seghers, 1966), p. 62.

26 Turk, *Child of Paradise*, p. 153.

27 Thiher, *Cinematic Muse*, p. 122.

28 Quoted in Elizabeth Grottle Strebel, 'French social cinema and the Popular Front', *Journal of Contemporary History* 12/3. (July 1977), p. 511.

29 Vincendeau, 'From the *bal populaire* to the casino', p. 52.

30 Françoise Garçon, *De Blum à Petain: Cinéma et société française (1936–1944)* (Paris: Éditions du Cerf, 1984), p. 53. The nine films Garçon identifies are *Le Crime de monsieur Lange*, *La Vie est à nous*, *Choc en retour* (1936), *La Bête humaine*, *Hôtel du Nord*, *Grisou* (1938), *Métropolitain* (1938), *Campement 13* (1939) and *Le Jour se lève*.

31 Hayward, *French National Cinema*, p. 153.

32 Crisp, *Genre, Myth, and Convention in the French Cinema*, p. 95.

33 Andrew, 'Poetic Realism', p. 117.

34 Ibid.

35 Crisp, *Genre, Myth, and Convention in the French Cinema*, p. xxiv.

36 Turk, *Child of Paradise*, pp. 162–3.

37 Vincendeau, *Stars and Stardom in French Cinema*, p. 70.

38 Ginette Vincendeau, 'Community, nostalgia and the spectacle of masculinity', *Screen* 26/6 (1985), p. 24.

39 Turk, *Child of Paradise*, p. 174.

40 Ibid., p. 158.

41 Robin Bates, 'Audiences on the verge of a Fascist breakdown: male anxieties and late 1930s French Film', *Cinema Journal* 36/3 (Spring 1997), p. 26.

42 Jean-Pierre Jeancolas, 'Cinéma des années trente: la crise et l'image de la crise', *Le Mouvement social* 154 (January–March 1991), p. 195.

43 Siegfried Kracauer, *From Caligari to Hitler: A Psychological Study of the German Film* (Princeton, NJ: Princeton University Press, 1947), p. 6.

44 Brett Bowles, 'Marcel Pagnol's *The Baker's Wife*: a cinematic charivari in Popular Front France', *The Historical Journal* 48/2 (2005), p. 468.

45 Susan Hayward, *Cinema Studies: The Key Concepts*, 3rd edn (London and New York: Routledge, 2006), p. 150.

46 Mark Cousins, *The Story of Film* (London: Pavilion, 2004), p. 162.

47 Dudley Andrew, *Mists of Regret: Culture and Sensibility in Classic French Film* (Princeton, NJ: Princeton University Press, 1995), p. 330.

4 Reception and Remake

A man walks about his room, moves a few things, lies on his bed, looks out of the window, chain-smokes […] and one is genuinely interested in him all the time (remembering afterwards that there exist directors who contrive to be boring even when they use fifteen characters in a motor car chase crackling with revolver shots).[1]

[These clapped-out hacks of surrealism] are all too anxious to take us wandering along the banks of canals, and to evoke for us the poignancy of bleak suburban wastelands, of rain-drenched villages […] and of piteous young girls caught up in anaemic dreams […] Never a true emotion, never a powerful feeling […] What I hold against them is that they got lost in as fog of literary allusions and of poetry for pallid realism.[2]

French reception

From a commercial point of view, *Le Jour se lève* did extremely well, premiering on 17 June 1939 at the Madeleine Theatre in Paris. Exact audience figures from this period are difficult to ascertain, given that normal cinema programming was greatly disrupted in the late summer and early autumn of 1939 as the widespread pressures of army mobilization and audience regulation sizes (due to fear of air raids) began to impact on exhibition practices. What we can be sure of is that its initial run was an unqualified commercial hit in Paris. It attracted 195,000 spectators in the first three months of release, and would have hypothetically amassed around 850,000 spectators by the end of 1939.[3] These figures reinforce Carné's popularity at the box office (*Hôtel du Nord* drew 695,000 spectators and *Le Quai des brumes* 854,000) and suggest that French audiences were engaged in 'collective spectacles of mourning',[4] drawn to those films that directly reflected their own sense of unease with the political climate of the late 1930s.

Yet while the film's commercial success was unambiguous, critical opinion from the outset was rigidly divided along political lines, indicative of the cultural politicization that had deepened in France throughout the 1930s. Accordingly, leftist publications like *L'Humanité*, *L'Avant-Garde*, *Ce soir* and *Ésprit* heralded *Le Jour se lève* as the most classically pure of Carné's 1930s films, applauding its strong performances, narrative ingenuity and darkly poetic sense of time and place. On the right, however, critics from *Action française*, *Je suis partout*, *Candide* and *Le Jour* all savagely denounced it as either demoralizing or aesthetically banal. For Christopher Faulkner, film reviewers in 1930s France consistently mobilized the issues of realism and naturalism to 'produce different aesthetic-social responses [...] with their differing political allegiances'.[5] Accordingly, throughout the late 1930s, critics from both sides of the political spectrum used Poetic Realist cinema, and Carné's films in particular, as a means of corroborating their own ideological positions. A closer examination of the positive and negative reaction to the film indicates how far French film criticism had become politicized by 1939.

Criticism of and praise for *Le Jour se lève* focused on two recurring aspects: the authenticity of the milieu and the ideological inflections of the populist subject matter. Writing in *Les Nouvelles littéraires* (17 June 1939), Alexandre Arnoux had already praised Carné in a 1936 review of *Jenny* as a 'name to remember' who possessed 'a sensitivity, an assuredness, an understanding of cinema, and an interior of strength that holds great promise'.[6] Of *Le Jour se lève*, Arnoux wrote approvingly of Carné's unique and continuing ability to 'create atmosphere' ('faire l'ambiance') but was less positive about the characters, who remained 'distant', 'estranged' and 'motiveless'.[7] Conversely, René Lehmann in *L'Intransigeant* noted how Carné depicts his characters 'with love, lucidity [...] and psychological precision' and admires his ability to intersect 'inexorable fatality' with recognizable character types and locales.[8] The leftist *Marianne* (21 June 1939) also praised the 'pleasant and tragic images' and the 'laudable Carné climate', and compared the narrative structure to those people who see their life pass before their eyes at the moment of death. The review was one of the few to note François's degrading work conditions, referring to the factory as 'apocalyptic'.[9] The right-wing critic Émile Vuillermoz – who had denounced *Le Quai des brumes* for depicting Frenchmen as derelicts and degenerates – began his review in *Le Temps* (17 June 1939) with: 'If you like your studies in morality to languish in darkness, if you like the seedy atmosphere of low-lives, if you like depictions of physical and moral misery, and if you like close contact with cruel destiny, then go and see *Le Jour se lève*.' Yet strangely, Vuillermoz proceeds to write glowingly of the film's poetic style and narrative complexities with terms like 'admirable', 'marvellous' and 'virtuosity'.[10] However, he concludes by ironically declaring: 'I wait impatiently for when day breaks ('le jour se lève') over less hopeless and despairing horizons.' So while there is little of the political hectoring that distinguishes many of the right-wing critical reviews, Vuillermoz's insistence that Carné should in future concentrate on less depressing subject matter reflects the growing clamour within French film discourse in the late 1930s for more consensual and analgesic narratives that would serve to mask the developing rifts within the body politic.

Indeed, at the other end of the political spectrum, negative right-wing reviews used Carné's predilection for 'ambiance' as a stick to beat the film mercilessly. Some resented the film's style – Jean Fayard set the tone in *Candide* (14 June 1939) by writing that the film 'is crammed full of useless images and looks a caricature of an old German film'. Worst still for Fayard was Carné's pretentiousness, for under the banner of populism, he argues that the film obliges the audience to swallow the 'worst kind of literature [where] no-one is sincere, no-one awakens our interest'.[11] Likewise, René Bizet accuses Carné both of simple cinematic recycling – 'We have seen this staircase in *Raskolnikov*, this factory in *Modern Times*, this manhunt in *Angels with Dirty Faces*' – and narrative portentousness, whereby the 'endless shots' of Gabin 'slow down the whole action'.[12] *Ordre* (22 June 1939) called *Le Jour se lève* a 'failed film' because, despite its surface quality, its 'slowness aggravates the spectator' and 'the studio design stinks of artificiality'.[13] The review's title, 'Why *Le Jour se lève* is heckled', is indicative of the right-wing critical discourse surrounding the film. And while James de Coquet in *Le Figaro* applauded the gentleness and sensitivity of the relationship between François and Françoise, he railed against the simplistic nature of the film, in which 'hard work is deemed bad [and] the police are treated as fools'. De Coquet's review is also one of the few to describe François's crime as what it is: cold-blooded murder.[14]

It was in the late 1930s that the expression *film noir* entered French cinematic discourse for the first time to describe the flourishing Poetic Realist style, and according to Charles O'Brien, rightist critics attributed to *noir* 'cultural connotations that were unambiguously negative'.[15] Right-wing film journals like *Action française*, *Je suis partout* and *Candide* frequently invoked *noir* as a pejorative catch-all phrase to denounce the moral conditions of

French cinematic praxis in the latter part of the 1930s. When *Le Quai des brumes* was awarded the *Grand prix national du cinéma français* in 1938, the editorial in *Le Petit Journal* did not fight too hard to hide its dismay at 'an immoral and demoralising *film noir*, whose effect on the public can only be harmful'.[16] For the likes of anti-Semitic critics like Lucien Rebatet (film critic for *Action française* between 1932 and 1939 and for *Je suis partout* from 1938 during the Occupation, under the pseudonym François Vinneuil), *Le Jour se lève* was the epitome of defeat, decadence and a cinema of perdition. His review in *Je suis partout* is worth quoting at length:

> I'm getting a little tired of dealing with the subject of this cinema of blood, of fog, and of mud. In the last two weeks, coming after so many others, one counts *Le Dernier Tournant* by Pierre Chenal and *Le Jour se lève* by Carné. These films have been reproached on moral grounds. With good reason. It seems not to have been observed, furthermore, that the genre blossomed at the same time of the Popular Front, that it only began to arouse protests with the decline of said Front, and that its principal representatives, such as Pierre Chenal and Carné, don't hide their Marxist tendencies. These films are unfortunate because they attach a sordid label to French cinema.[17]

Rebatet's rejection of this 'cinema of blood, of fog, and of mud' had first emerged in a 1936 review of *Jenny*, where he vehemently objected to the film's political and populist convictions and its 'stale and corny brasserie Baudelairism'.[18] Whereas Communist critic Georges Sadoul had described the new emergent strain of cinematic 'populist realism' exemplified by Carné's films as 'an understanding of the world that is ours [...] a sense of revolt against the society which has produced this inhuman world',[19] Rebatet and other right-wing cinema critics despised these films' decadent cosmopolitanism and degrading determinism, blaming their existence on foreigners, Communists and Jews. Many negative reviews of Carné's films employed metaphors of disease, dirt (*Le Quai des brumes* was populated with 'cowards, larvae [and] asocial creatures'[20]) and unmanliness (*Hôtel du Nord*'s 'slack, flabby populism' was denounced by Rebatet[21]). *Le Jour se lève* was regarded as dangerous precisely because it did not propose an analgesic corroboration of France's cohesion and renewal promised by the restoration of the conservative government. Instead, *Le Jour se lève* reflects back to audiences an image of itself, and as such embodies a form of social and cultural resistance that critics like Rebatet cannot afford to sanction. As Faulkner makes clear, '[t]hrough seeing themselves, working-class people could be led to a dangerous knowledge of themselves and their social conditions'.[22] It was far safer then, for those on the right, to mobilize a discourse of xenophobia and pronounce films like *Le Jour se lève* as 'sordid' and driven by Jewish motivations.

The most celebrated review of the film was written by Georges Altman in *La Lumière*. Entitled '*Le Jour se lève*: A pure *film noir*' ['Un film noir mais propre'], Altman defends the film against the accusations of 'vacationing vaudeville writers' and commends its 'excruciatingly gloomy' and 'perfectly pure' aesthetic, comparing it to 'the subversive power of a dream or a bomb'.[23] The review reads like an extended recapitulation of Poetic Realist cinema's concerns and preoccupations, invoking references to Baudelaire, G.W. Pabst, *I Am a Fugitive from a Chain Gang* (1932), Francis Carco, Ibsen and Offenbach. For Altman, the film represents the pinnacle of the whole Poetic Realist project, where 'crime, suicide, and suffering take on a naked simplicity' and the entire working class is etched onto the face of Jean Gabin. And yet for Altman, the film is 'no longer a matter of a revolver, a crime, a "milieu"'. In other words, it is part of, but also detached from, its cinematic antecedents. This is French *noir* at its most distilled, full of the tropes that anticipate the American version of the term (the 'one long night' scenario, the decor imbued with fatalistic overtones, the inexorability of the narrative trajectory).

Blame the barometer?

Facing the threat of war, and aware of the subversive potential of cinema to satirize state institutions like the Church and the Army, Edouard Daladier's recently elected French government moved quickly to establish a Commissariat de l'Information [Department of Information] in 1938. Though the extent of its powers was hazy, the body's chief function by late 1939 was to oversee film censorship. After war broke out in September, the Department censors – who had earlier called upon French directors to make 'healthy and optimistic' films – identified 56 films as 'difficult [...] painful [...] derisory [...] depressing, morbid, and immoral'.[24] As might be expected, films such as *La Grande Illusion*, *La Règle du jeu*, *Le Dernier Tournant* and *Les Bas-Fonds* – as well as *Hôtel du Nord* and *Le Quai des brumes* – were deemed demoralizing and defeatist and were immediately banned. This was by no means the end of the scapegoating. The French military high command, anxious to avoid equating France's fall to their own professional unpreparedness, held doggedly to cultural explanations to exculpate their own shortcomings. 'If we have lost the war, it is because of *Le Quai des brumes*,[25] declared various Vichy spokesmen, corroborating the misgivings of military censors who saw in Carné's films recurring motifs of powerlessness and emasculation. Rather than France's fall explicated by the German army's improved operational capabilities, and inefficient domestic intelligence-gathering and chaotic policy-making in the later 1930s (which are far more accurate conclusions), Vichy adduced Carné's films – along with André Gide and *congés payés* – for contributing to the 1940 debacle. Carné's reply – that the barometer cannot be blamed for the storm it foretells – indicates the extent to which *Le Jour se lève* had become an ideological battleground for the political, social and emotional tribulations taking place in France in the last 18 months of the 1930s. Whereas the right-wing press had initially seen the film as an articulation of a growing strand of proletarian populism in French cultural life, its entire aesthetic was now conveniently admonished for precipitating France's fall. Poetic Realist cinema was blamed by Vichy civil servants for 'represent[ing] our country, our traditions, our race, with a face altered, lying, deformed by an artistic prism which, while often original, isn't always sane'.[26] Such condemnatory hysteria was a continuation of the explicit rightist discourses of the late 1930s, and fed into a patriotic Pétainist film culture which encouraged the depiction of authoritarian father figures, the assertive restoration of masculine values, and the relegation of the working-class to the representational margins.

Yet while it is true that after the imposition of strict cultural policies by the Vichy government in late 1939 and early 1940, screenings of *Le Jour se lève* were severely limited, the film was never banned outright. Carné states as much, recalling that the film 'slowly but surely reappeared' in late 1940 after it was re-classified for audiences over the age of sixteen due to the film's openness with issues of sexual freedom. The only direct intervention from censorship authorities was to remove the shot of the naked Arletty partially hidden behind a shower curtain (a shot that has never been restored).[27] Christopher Faulkner notes that *Semaine à Paris* afforded high praise to the film in January 1941, that it was rereleased in September 1941 and that it was showing in nearly 30 different exhibition venues up until at least September 1943. Banning of the film was ad hoc rather than systematic, and only really gathered pace after the return of Pierre Laval to power in April 1942 and the rapid German invasion of the southern Vichy zone in November 1942. It appears, then, that a surprising number of films and a number of surprising films seem to have suffered no ill effects until very late in the Occupation, which in turn reignites the debate over clandestine film culture and questions the level of cultural blackout imposed by the Germans.

What is clear is that the imperatives of Vichy cultural practice sought to connect art to the political exigencies of the time. The Occupation meant the imposition of a different kind of cinema. Realism – poetic, social, or otherwise – was out, and films were now obliged to conform to a heavily constructed, politically motivated nationalistic discourse summed up by Pétain's National Revolution slogan of 'Family, Fatherland, Work'. If 1930s Poetic Realism was a cinema 'conjugated in the present tense',[28] then Carné's two wartime films opted, like many films made between 1940 and 1944, for historical recreation. *Les Visiteurs du soir* was a fairy-tale romance set in the Middle Ages and *Les Enfants du paradis* took place in an 1840s Paris populated by real characters of the time. This applied recreation of historical characters and place was a necessary stratagem in the face of German edicts on subject matter and style. So while both may look deliberately theatrical, retrograde even, they were nevertheless greatly indebted to the tenets of Poetic Realism.[29]

International reception

Le Jour se lève – translated for English-speaking audiences as *Daybreak* – was released in America on 29 July 1940. As in France, critical reception was somewhat ambivalent during its limited American release, with reviews unsure whether to praise or pan the film's technical mastery, emotional heft and nihilistic undertones. The Paris correspondent for *Variety* had reviewed the film a year earlier on its initial French release (26 July 1939) and had complained then that 'an otherwise excellent theme is marred by some basic errors of psychology which a more careful study of the human character would have avoided'. The review criticized the miscasting of Laurent and also felt Gabin to be 'too much the Gabin of every picture to date'. However, it did single out Arletty's and Jules Berry's performances for praise, as well as the cinematography and score, judging the film to be 'another of the series of psychological studies in which French directors specialize'.[30] Bosley Crowther in *The New York Times* (30 July 1940) also began his review by recognizing how the film was representative of a particular type of French film, noting the 'morbid preoccupation of certain French film producers [...] with characters who live in cold-water walk-ups and go crazy and do violent things'. Crowther praised Gabin's performance ('the most hunted and haunted actor in French cinema') and Carné's handling of the suspense aspect for the first three-quarters of the film. 'Then,' he writes, 'the motivation falters, an anticlimax sets in. The pity of it all seems slightly forced, the melodramatics too obvious.'³¹ On the surface, Joseph F. Coughlan at the *Motion Picture Herald* (3 August 1940) is even more negative, criticizing the film as 'dreary and depressing' and a 'dirgeful requiem chord [...] too sour to stomach'. But Gabin is again mentioned as 'the first choice of French casting offices for portraying harassed humanity', and there is positive appreciation of the music, cinematography and performances. What is more, Coughlan ends by mentioning that the performance was very well attended, and that viewers watched 'the mournful meanderings [...] with evident absorption, except for small titters that ran through the audience in the form of nervous reaction as the plot screwed more tightly'.³² By far the most positive American review appeared in *Time* (19 August 1940), which described *Daybreak* as 'perhaps the last major product of a cinema industry that was as long on brains as it was short on budget'. The review concluded: 'It has the same distinguishing Gallic qualities of artistic shrewdness and spirited disenchantment that make most Hollywood pictures by comparison seem, for better or worse, not quite grown up'.³³

In Britain, where the film was not released until 1944, the *Monthly Film Bulletin* applauded a film 'rich in the artistry of true cinema', and included remarks that neatly articulate the entire French Poetic Realist sensibility: a 'delicate tenderness' combined with a 'realistic, fatalistic emphasis on the tawdry'.³⁴ As screenings of the film became more frequent after the war, more and more American and British critics discovered *Le Jour se lève* – and the rest of the Poetic Realist corpus – and lavished considerable praise upon it. Pauline Kael in *The New Yorker* called it 'the finest of the French poetic melodramas',³⁵ while Dilys Powell, renowned for her career-long admiration of the 'Frenchness' of French cinema, wrote nostalgically in *The Sunday Times* how Poetic Realism's focus on 'people with a deep and tender feeling for the under-side of life, the shadowed pavement of the street [and] the human unfortunate' has created French national cinema's 'best films on the theme of undisciplined life'.³⁶ The most passionate review of the film in the British press was undoubtedly by Roger Manvell in *Sight & Sound*. Manvell used the release of the American remake (see below) to enhance the reputation of the original, describing it as the best of the Carné-Prévert collaborations and an 'intense, dynamic, human and moving tragedy'.³⁷

Le Jour se lève – and Poetic Realism more generally – was emblematic of a certain type of film that the American film industry in particular was seeking to imitate. In March 1939, as *Le Jour se lève* was being filmed, famed Hollywood producer David O. Selznick sent a memorandum to William

Cameron Menzies, Lyle Wheeler and Edward Boyle, the design team he had assembled for *Gone with the Wind*:

> There has been a great deal of comment recently about the difference between the outstanding French pictures, and the American pictures, in that the better French pictures seem to capture a quality of reality in the photography, sets, and costumes that is lacking even in the best American pictures. I personally feel that this criticism is a justifiable one. I feel that our sets always look exactly what they are – sets that have been put up a few hours before, instead of seeming in their ageing and in their dressing to be rooms that have existed for some time and have been lived in.[38]

Selznick's aspiration to create 'lived-in' sets is a trenchant reminder of the attention French cinema has always placed on decor and design, and in the context of the 1930s it suggests that an exportable vision of French cinema – exemplified by 'the outstanding French pictures' – is represented by films that the rest of the world was aspiring to emulate. As producer Pierre Braunberger wrote: 'Poetic Realism, whether good or bad, gave glory to French cinema and was sold around the world [...] nobody makes this movie better than the French.'[39] At the same time, British novelist and film critic Graham Greene echoed Selznick's observations when he wrote that the best French directors of the period were those who possessed 'the trick of presenting a more intimate reality'.[40] Greene applauded the authenticity of a design scheme (he was writing about *Hôtel du Nord*) that seemed loaded with emotional possibilities. Noting the revival of several Poetic Realist films in London cinemas, Gavin Lambert's two 1948 articles for *Sequence* – one on 'The New Pessimism' in post-war French cinema, the other on Carné's pre-war films – reinforced *Le Jour se lève*'s cultural cachet. For Lambert, the film 'has a compactness that gives it perfection', and was made by 'a dramatic poetic of those eternal *maladies des villes* unequalled by any director'.[41] *Le Jour se lève*, then, possessed both a 'lived-in' quality (the 'Realist') and an evocative atmospheric sheen (the 'Poetic'). This explains in part why virtually every international review commented on the expressiveness of the film's design, the painstaking faithfulness to reality and its 'wooful, but also very woeful'[42] undertones. As we saw in Chapter 1, the over-representation of pre-war Poetic Realist films across the international exhibition circuits in the immediate aftermath of the Liberation accounts for these films' historical sustainability. As encapsulated by Italo Calvino's famous dictum – that 'French cinema of the 1930s smelled of real odours, as opposed to the Palmolive of American cinema'[43] – Poetic Realism, and *Le Jour se lève*, became the critically sanctioned representatives of French film history.

Le Jour se lève remade – 'As dark as a Hallmark card?'

In 1950, Bazin wrote the following:

> In nearly all Gabin films – at least from *La Bête humaine* to *Au-delà des grilles* – he comes to a violent end that has the appearance, more or less, of suicide [...] But can you see Gabin as a family man? Could anyone imagine that, at the end of *Le Quai des Brumes*, he had managed to snatch poor Michèle Morgan from the clutches of Michel Simon and Pierre Brasseur, and sailed with her to a future in America; or that, having come to his senses, he preferred when day broke in *Le Jour se lève* to turn himself in and hope for a probable acquittal?[44]

Le Jour se lève's afterlife was prolonged by the RKO American remake of the film in 1947 which indeed provided the very 'happy end' that Bazin was mocking. As *The Long Night* closes, Jo Ann manages to evade the police, get into the apartment and see Joe.[45] He almost shoots her, but then agrees to leave with her and they face the police arm-in-arm. *The Long Night* was directed by Anatole Litvak from a John Wexley screenplay and starred Henry Fonda (as Joe Adams [François]), Vincent Price (as Maximilian [Valentin]), Barbara Bel Geddes (as Jo Ann [François]) and Ann Dvorak (as Charlene [Clara]). Some changes are unobtrusive (Maximilian is a magician, not an animal trainer), others more unsettling (Litvak includes excerpts from the second movement of Beethoven's Seventh Symphony), but by far the most egregious alteration for critics was the new redemptive ending, where the assembled crowd shout their support for Joe as he emerges from the apartment to face the police.

Le Jour se lève was not the only 1930s French film to be remade in America at this time. Others include *La Chienne* (Jean Renoir, 1931) into *Scarlet Street* (Fritz Lang, 1945), *Pépé le Moko* into *Algiers* (John Cromwell, 1938) and then *Casbah* (John Berry, 1948), *La Bête humaine* into *Human Desire* (Fritz Lang, 1954) and *Pièges* (Robert Siodmak, 1939) into *Lured* (Douglas Sirk, 1947).[46] Although these remakes are all clearly working within a different set of industrial, aesthetic and ideological contexts, when it comes to subject of American remakes of French films, Carolyn A. Durham's comments are instructive:

> either they [the American films] embody American culture and its dominance and so threaten to erase any trace of foreign influence that they might encounter along their imperialist path, or they represent foolish and futile attempts to reproduce a foreign model whose cultural and aesthetic specificity [...] make it, by definition, inimitable.[47]

For Durham, these remakes seek to accommodate the original text within a new set of cultural, social and political discourses, and the resulting reorientation usually leads to an inferior product. The acute strains of anti-Americanism that frequently emerged whenever popular European films were remade in Hollywood were highlighted by the reaction of one editorial in a British newspaper:

> Purchase by Hollywood of that magnificent French picture, *Le Jour se lève*, is ominous. They propose to remake the whole thing in bigger and bouncier form [...] This is a fate worse than death. It is akin to the horrible American habit of pulling flowers to pieces and rearranging the petals to make them look more 'attractive'.[48]

This tone continued in a comparison of the two films in *L'Écran français* entitled '*Le Jour se lève* – "remade" and betrayed'. Claude Bower continued by arguing that that the practice of uprooting and transplanting French films into an American context only led to films 'deprived of their authenticity, emasculated, and bastardised'.[49] Bower concluded that 'all that Carné and Prévert suggested with a gesture, a phrase, a look, Anatole Litvak sprawled out with grand discursive reinforcements and blundering explanations'.[50]

Critics were not just fearful of a diluted cultural product, but also condemned the frequent Hollywood practice of purchasing the rights to the original films and then taking them out of distribution and destroying them. Thus, the National Film Library was only allowed to hold a copy of *Le Jour se lève* on the strict proviso that it would never be shown until permission was given by the new rights-holder, RKO. As Tom Brown puts it, RKO's attempts to destroy *Le Jour se lève* both economically and physically was reflected in *The Daily Worker*'s response to the remake as 'lifeless', a 'ghost' and a 'film which is dead'.[51]

The Long Night's tagline is revealing – 'Love that promised the world [...] and paid off in bullets!' This commonly framed discourse is designed to corroborate coordinates familiar to the thriller and the romance. Moreover, classical Hollywood cinema's tendency towards greater narrative exposition and transparency is clear from the opening scenes of *The Long Night*. Textual and tonal differences emerge immediately: the film begins with a documentary-style montage of shots depicting cities of heavy industry, while a ponderous voice-over names them – 'Gary, Indiana', 'Bethlehem, Pennsylvania' and 'Youngstown, Ohio'. The camera then fixes on a final skyline – a mill town in the Pennsylvania-West Virginia area – and the narrator informs us that the name of this particular town is not important, rather the universality of the story. Litvak's decision to embrace such specificity pulls away the skein of poetry that envelopes *Le Jour se lève* so tightly. Hollywood's insistence upon narrative clarity and more sustained exposition means that character motivation in *The Long Night* is explicitly foregrounded. For instance, Brown notes that while the audience is told that François is the landlady's best tenant, Joe is shown playing with a neighbour's child and stroking a cat. These strategies thus 'neutralise ambiguity' and 'streamline characterisation' so that the psychological complexity of the original is excised.[52]

Furthermore, *The Long Night* diverges from its source text in its treatment of class and social relations. Whereas *Le Jour se lève* prioritized class conflict and work as important aspects of late-1930s French society, class discourses are marginalized in the remake to be superseded by a war discourse. Later on, when Joe shouts down to the crowd from his window, there is no mention of 'le sable' that François refers to, even though both work in a sandblasting factory. Instead, Joe refers to the war – he has 'seen plenty of killers' and 'plenty killed'. Of course, RKO's decision to shed the original's ideological convictions has resultant ideological consequences of its own. By removing all references to the unhealthiness of work (even Jo Ann's flowers do not wither when she meets Joe), *The Long Night* does not seek to critique America's post-war economic situation – as the billboard says, 'Peace and Prosperity'. Rather, as Vincendeau observes, 'class is reduced to being "from the wrong side of the tracks" and class oppression is "universalised" into war trauma'.[53] So, Joe's status as a returning US soldier from World War II is invoked several times in the opening sequences of the film, creating audience sympathy and identification, and investing the film with a very different set of ideological inclinations. The experience of war rather than class solidarity is privileged, to the extent that the mayor criticizes the police chief over his treatment of Joe: 'Don't you see you're making him a hero, like he were holding off a bunch of Japs', and the murder of Maximilian is equated with the morally acceptable killing of Germans during the war.

American critic James Agee wrote how both films 'clearly rate themselves as tragedies; they are merely intelligent trash'; he did admit, however, that *Le Jour se lève* 'is much more discreet with its self-pity and much more sharply edged'.[54] Critics objected to the film's style (*The New York Times* disparaged the 'clickety-clack of talk, talk, talk'[55]), universally regarding it as inferior to the quiet moments of introspection running through *Le Jour se lève*. However, the critical slamming of *The Long Night* – and of American remakes of French films more generally – is not particularly helpful in unpacking the differences between source and hybrid text. Instead, it is more productive to view the remake's apparent ideological and artistic compromises and its historical unmooring in terms of cultural transfer and the differences between French and Hollywood censorship and moral codes. *The Long Night* may feel less resonant, but the historical determinants of both films were vastly different – a France in social and political turmoil on the eve of war, an America on the cusp of a post-war economic boom. Because *The Long Night* does not follow through the 'fatalistic thrust' of *Le Jour se lève* and its 'incompatibility with the real world',[56] the remake's happy end should be read more as an ideological validation of American triumphalism and heroism (as with *The Long Night*, both *Human Desire* and *The 13th Letter*, Otto Preminger's 1951 remake of Clouzot's *Le Corbeau* [1943] transform the lead character into a returning war veteran). In each case, flawed characters can be rehabilitated or recuperated through a streamlined war discourse. Finally, the presence of Litvak in the American remake conveniently emphasizes the transnational aesthetic fluidity that links *Le Jour se lève* and *The Long Night*. Litvak's double-émigré trajectory, from Russia to Paris to Hollywood, coupled with his stylistic successes in France (*Mayerling* [1936]) and his development of the *noir* idiom in an American context (alongside *Out of the Fog* [1941] and *Sorry, Wrong Number* [1948]), exemplify the persistent ideological and industrial negotiations at play between source and duplicate cinematic texts.

Afterlife I: whatever happened to Marcel Carné?

In the early 1950s, Carné's reputation began to diminish dramatically and despite the burnished success of *Les Enfants du paradis* he never again reached the sustained heights of his 1930s output. This was due to numerous factors: being seen as an orchestrator of multiple talents rather than a true auteur like Renoir; his decision to stay in France during the Occupation was seen as a tacit acceptance of Vichy; the end of his creative partnership with Prévert in 1949 and his inability to adapt to the changing nature of the post-war film industry. *Les Portes de la nuit* in particular was admonished for its nostalgic embracing of a Poetic Realist aesthetic that had, by 1946, become 'all too familiar and predictable'.[57] Moreover, by building a full-scale replica of the Barbès-Rochechouart Métro station, he was criticized for financial profligacy at a time of national austerity.[58] No matter that *Les Portes de la nuit* was a commercial success (it was seen by 2.6 million spectators, 800,000 of them in Paris, and actually outgrossed *Martin Roumagnac*, the eagerly anticipated Gabin-Dietrich film that *Les Portes de la nuit* was meant to have been[59]), the perception was – and would remain for the rest of his career – that Carné's glittering successes of the 1930s and early 1940s were an aberration and could best be summed up by Claude Mauriac's acid remark: 'It is not Carné who has declined; it is we who, from the start, overestimated him.'[60]

Bazin's 1951 article 'The Disincarnation of Carné' expanded this discourse by noting that the studio-bound excesses of Carné's pre-war films looked decidedly unmodern in a post-war climate that had necessitated new themes and visual styles. Bazin argued that Carné had 'a knack for crystallizing all the widespread harshness and criticism',[61] especially given the savage reception that had greeted Carné's *Juliette, ou la clef des songes* at the 1951 Cannes Film Festival. Around the same time, Italian neo-realist director Roberto Rossellini suggested that Carné should 'free himself a little from the straitjacket of the studio, and get out more and look more closely at the man in the street'.[62] This was a deeply ironic statement given Carné's call to filmmakers in the early 1930s to 'go down the streets' and capture the essence of the urban experience. Rossellini's comments clarify how filmmaking praxis had changed after the end of World War II. The aesthetic of 'closed' filmmaking, exemplified by *Le Jour se lève*, with its emphasis on studio design and rigid determinism, had been usurped by the neo-realist aesthetics of René Clément's *La Bataille du rail* (1946) and Rossellini's *Rome, Open City* (1948), films that emphasized documentary-style reportage and spontaneity. By pinpointing the extent to which Carné's preoccupations with the artifice of studio-based filming took precedence over freedom, Rossellini was articulating an unwarranted criticism of Carné that sadly remains to this day.

All this came at a time, too, when *Cahiers du cinéma* critics like François Truffaut and Jean-Luc Godard were advocating a radical break with France's pre-war studio aesthetic. Carné's thematic and visual conventions were very much 'of their own time' in comparison to the self-regenerating and self-reinventing aspects of other post-war national film praxis, and the perceived failure of *Les Portes de la nuit* signalled French filmmaking's definitive rupture with the dominant production values of the 1930s towards the *Nouvelle Vague* terrain of spontaneous guerrilla-style filmmaking. In many ways, Carné's fall from grace in post-war French cultural circles allegorizes the changes in approach to film 'realism' between the 1930s and the 1950s. As we have seen, it was a rare review of Carné's films in the 1930s that neglected to mention the beauty and verisimilitude of the *mise-en-scène*. His films offered an exportable version of French cinema in the 1930s that concentrated on plastic values and the importance of mood and atmosphere, yet it was this very dependency upon 'plasticity' – studio-controlled set design and lighting

– that smacked of aesthetic bankruptcy, inauthenticity and 'meretricious academicism'[63] for post-war film critics like Truffaut.

Yet it is just not true that Carné suffered a professional decline after *Les Enfant du paradis*. As we saw, *Les Portes de la nuit* was a success. His *noir*ish *Thérèse Raquin* won the second-prize Silver Lion at the 1953 Venice Film Festival and he was still working with Gabin, too – on reasonable successes *La Marie du port* (1950) and *L'Air de Paris* (1954). *Les Tricheurs* won the Grand Prix du Cinéma in 1958, and was the highest-grossing film of the 1958–59 season (with remarkable Paris box-office figures of over 556,000). Moreover, Carné was not collectively assassinated by *Cahiers du cinéma*, for before Truffaut's mid-1950s broadsides, Jacques Doniol-Valcroze had written a balanced 1953 article, detailing 'the natural mark of a great director'.[64] Much later, in 1979, he received a special César award to honour *Les Enfants du paradis* as 'the best French film in the history of talking pictures'. This marked the apotheosis of Carné's career, forever consecrating that film as a canonical work in world cinema.

Carné also received a major fillip in 1989 with the publication of Edward Baron Turk's penetrating study, *Child of Paradise: Marcel Carné and the Golden Age of French Cinema*. The book radically recuperated Carné after his fall from grace, and now placed him at the apex of the French tradition of classical filmmaking. Through a nuanced combination of close film analysis and the intersection of wider cultural production and political factors, Turk's Cultural Studies approach paints a picture of Carné as France's 'most demanding, irascible, and invincible film director'.[65] Two aspects of the book are worth discussing. Firstly, Turk argues that Carné's entire cinematic universe is predicated on the Freudian concept of the 'primal scene', in which a child accidentally observes his parents having sexual relations. Each of Carné's films contains a variation of the primal scene, a situation 'in which one character inadvertently intrudes on the intimacy of two others',[66] which leads to feelings of disillusionment, incompletion and unfulfilled desire. Examples include Dany spying on her mother through black curtains in *Jenny* and Lacenaire pulling back a drape to reveal to the gathered guests Baptiste and Garance in each other's arms in *Les Enfants du paradis*. In *Le Jour se lève*, there are two primal scenes – Valentin's eavesdropping, and the whole of the film from the first gunshots to the penultimate scene. Secondly, the study is highly innovative in that Turk acknowledges for the first time Carné's concealed homosexuality, and shows how this colours the gender and sexual politics in his films. Alongside other biographical elements – the attributing of Carné's pessimistic tone to the early death of his mother, for instance – Turk argues that Carné's repressed homosexuality is reflected thematically throughout his entire oeuvre, and that characters in each of his films, from *Jenny* (1936) to *La Merveilleuse Visite* (1974) 'seek ceaselessly to break from the claustrophobia of their physical and spiritual environment and return to an early paradise'.[67] Turk also shows how characters in Carné's films often negotiate gender codes (like Nelly in *Le Quai des brumes* or Baptiste in *Les Enfants du paradis*), and concludes that had Carné been more explicit in his treatment of the homoerotic in his films (like Jean Cocteau had), the likes of Truffaut may have championed Carné rather than reject him. The potential interface between Poetic Realism's dark pessimism and Carné's queerness sheds an intriguing light on previous readings of Poetic Realism, and opened up new ways of analysing Carné for critics like Richard Dyer, Noël Burch and Geneviève Sellier. Although Turk's approach impacts less on *Le Jour se lève* than on, say, *L'Air de Paris* (described by Dyer as 'an early example of an explicitly homosexual mainstream feature film'[68]), Turk still exposes implicit homosexual overtones in the struggle between François and Valentin, describing their cat-and-mouse scene in François's apartment 'as a kind of foreplay to the rough skirmish by the window'.[69] Turk's epilogue – 'It is perhaps inevitable that a film director who portrays life's essential loneliness will fail to command universal assent'[70] – gets to the heart of the Carné post-war enigma.

Afterlife II: the rise and rise of *Le Jour se lève*

The rising reputation of Carné's best film, however, was far less of an enigma than the decline of its director. The beginnings of *Le Jour se lève*'s robust afterlife were due in no small part to Bazin, who resurrected the film from widespread neglect and RKO's suppressions in his acclaimed *Ciné-club* analysis, first distributed to film clubs in 1947 and published more widely in 1950. He nostalgically observed how, by the start of the 1950s, the film represented 'the ideal qualities of a cinematic paradise lost',[71] and his analysis paid close attention to more than just the usual exploration of narrative, performance and theme to which film criticism routinely limited itself.

In America, critics began to notice the commonalities between French Poetic Realism and their own *noir* tradition. The traditional discourse established by Raymonde Borde and Étienne Chaumenton in their 1955 pioneering study of *film noir* was one that underplayed the relationship between the two styles. In *Panorama du film noir américain*, they asked: 'Did *Pépé le Moko*,

Le Quai des brumes, La Bête humaine foreshadow the American *film noir*? We don't think so.'[72] Borde and Chaumenton minimized the importance of the visual textures of the French Poetic Realist style exemplified by *Le Jour se lève* – 'the poetry of wet cobblestones, of nights in the *faubourgs* and of bleak dawns' – despite sharing this iconography with American *noir*. Yet in a move away from this cultural reductionism, the notion that *noir* was the product of the complex interface between French and American national praxis began to gain cultural purchase. For American playwright and director David Mamet, *Le Jour se lève* gave Hollywood audiences a very un-American view of crime. 'Our crime films', he wrote, 'are, in the main, romances, celebrating either camaraderie (the gangster film) or freedom (the *film noir*) [...] *Le Jour se lève*, however, is not a crime romance, but something of a crime tragedy, or a tragedy of guilt'.[73] The throughlines in this gradual transatlantic shift from Poetic Realism to *policier* were thus both stable (visual, cinematographic) and changeable (narratives of doom and gloom replaced by lights at the end of tunnels).

Poetic Realism and *film noir* also shared a common approach to the possibilities or otherwise of agency; in the French context, argues Mark Bould, 'regardless of what you do on the train, it is still going to pull into the same station'; whereas in American *noir*, the protagonists 'lay the tracks themselves'.[74] François's speech in the greenhouse ('The trams all go by [...] But now you're with me, everything's going to be different') anticipates much of the fatalism and psychological trauma of American post-war *noir* and reveals the extent of the stylistic and narrational debts owed to late-1930s French cinema.

Slowly but surely, *Le Jour se lève* achieved a sustained level of critical and cultural respectability. In 1952, the first of *Sight & Sound*'s ten-yearly polls to establish the Ten Best Films ranked *Le Jour se lève* equal seventh, alongside *Greed* (1924) and *The Passion of Joan of Arc* (1928).[75] At the World Fair in Brussels in 1958, Jacques Ledoux and the Belgian Cinémathèque polled 117 historians from 26 countries for 'The Best Films of All Time'; this time *Le Jour se lève* ranked 38th. More recently, in November 2007, *Cahiers du cinéma* published its list of '100 films pour une cinémathèque idéale', and ranked *Le Jour se lève* joint 90th on the list alongside such eclectic company as *Mulholland Drive* (2001), *The Bicycle Thieves* (1948) and *Letter from an Unknown Woman* (1948). Contemporary French cinema has absorbed the film's visual fabric, with Sylvain Chomet's *Les Triplettes de Belleville* (2003) overflowing with allusions to Carné's 1930s films, right down to the vertiginous apartment block that reclaims Trauner's original. Christopher Barratier's

Faubourg 36 (2008) revisits and recycles the iconography of *Le Jour se lève*, while Jean-Pierre Darroussin's Paul, who calmly shoots co-workers at the start of *De bon matin* (2011) and then sits in his office and waits for the police to arrive, is a modern-day François. And aren't those delicate webs of fate in *Le Fabuleux Destin d'Amélie Poulain* (2001) just updated versions of Carné's particular brand of determinism that has a hold over all his characters? And so *Le Jour se lève* lives on.

Notes

1   Richard Winnington, 'A slight case of murder' (11 May 1946), repr. in *Drawn and Quartered* (London: Saturn, 1948), p. 54.
2   Jean-Georges Auriol, writing in 1941, referring to the plots and characters of Poetic Realism. Quoted in Colin Crisp, *Genre, Myth, and Convention in the French Cinema, 1929–1939* (Bloomington: Indiana University Press, 2002), p. 246.
3   Crisp, *Genre, Myth, and Convention in the French Cinema*, p. 333. Crisp provides two figures for *Le Jour se lève*: one for the actual entry figures before the outbreak of war (195,000) and one for the estimated final audience number had the film's release circumstances been normal (850,000).
4   Brett Bowles, 'Marcel Pagnol's *The Baker's Wife*: a cinematic charivari in Popular Front France', *The Historical Journal* 48/2 (2005), p. 439.
5   Christopher Faulkner, 'Theory and practice of film reviewing in France in the 1930s: eyes right (Lucien Rebatet and *Action française* 1936–1939)', *French Cultural Studies* 3/8 (June 1992), p. 151.
6   In Edward Baron Turk, *Child of Paradise: Marcel Carné and the Golden Age of French Cinema* (Cambridge, MA, and London: Harvard University Press, 1989), p. 69.
7   Alexandre Arnoux, '*Le Jour se lève*', *Les Nouvelles littéraires* (17 June 1939), p. 10.
8   Cited in Michel Pérez, *Les Films de Carné* (Paris: Ramsay, 1986), p. 65.
9   Mezzanine, '*Le Jour se lève*', *Marianne* (21 June 1939), p. 19.
10   Émile Vuillermoz, '*Le Jour se lève*', *Le Temps* (17 June 1939), p. 5.
11   Jean Fayard, '*Le Jour se lève*', *Candide* (14 June 1939), p. 17.
12   René Bizet, '*Le Jour se lève*', *L'Écho de Paris* (11 June 1939), n.p.
13   Paul Achard, 'Pourquoi est sifflé *Le Jour se lève*', *Ordre* (22 June 1939), n.p.
14   James de Coquet, '*Le Jour se lève*', *Le Figaro* (14 June 1939), p. 4.
15   Charles O'Brien, 'Film noir in France: before the liberation', *Iris* 21 (Spring 1996), p. 8.
16   Cited in ibid., p. 10.
17   Cited in Christopher Faulkner, 'Critical debate and the construction of society', in Michael Temple and Michael Witt (eds), *The French Cinema Book* (London: BFI, 2004), p. 175.
18   Rebatet, '*Jenny*', *Action française*, <http://www.marcel-carne.com/filmographie/jenny.html#revue> (accessed 1 March 2009).
19   Faulkner, 'Critical debate and the construction of society', p. 175.
20   *La Cinématographie française* (May 1938), cited in Faulkner, 'Critical debate and the construction of society', p. 174.
21   Rebatet, 'L'écran de la semaine: *La Bête humaine*', *Action française* (30 December 1938), n.p.
22   Faulkner, 'Theory and practice of film reviewing', p. 152.
23   Georges Altman, '*Le Jour se lève*: une œuvre noire et pure', *La Lumière* (16 June 1939), p. 5
24   Suzanne Borel, untitled editorial, *La Cinématographie française*, 1093 (14 October 1939).
25   Cited by Marcel Carné, *La Vie à belles dents* (Paris: Pierre Belfond, 1989), p. 126.

26   Cited in Claude Gauteur, *Jean Renoir: La Double Méprise 1925-1939* (Paris: Les Éditeurs français réunis), p. 141.

27   Carné, *La Vie à belles dents*, p. 126.

28   Jean-Pierre Jeancolas, 'Beneath the despair, the show goes on: Marcel Carné's *Les Enfants du paradis* (1943-5)', trans. Marianne Johnson, in Susan Hayward and Ginette Vincendeau (eds), *French Film: Texts and Contexts*, 2nd edn (London and New York: Routledge, 2000), p. 78.

29   In the autumn of 1939 Carné began pre-production on his next project, *École communale*. Henri Jeanson and Jacques Prévert were working on scripts and dialogue, Trauner and Jaubert had been hired, and Arletty, Pierre Lenoir and Corinne Luchaire had been offered lead roles. Little is known about the film and Carné certainly did not return to it after the Occupation.

30   Anon., '*Daybreak*', *Variety* (26 July 1939), p. 503.

31   Bosley Crowther, '*Daybreak*', *The New York Times* (30 July 1940), n.p.

32   Joseph L. Coughlan, '*Daybreak*', *Motion Picture Herald* (3 August 1940), p. 42.

33   Anon., '*Daybreak*', *Time* (19 August 1940), n.p.

34   Anon., '*Daybreak*', *Monthly Film Bulletin* 21/132 (1944), p. 47.

35   Pauling Kael, *5001 Nights at the Movies* (New York and London: Marion Boyars, 1993), p. 383.

36   Dilys Powell, 'Since 1939', repr. in Christopher Cook (ed.), *The Dilys Powell Film Reader* (Manchester: Carcanet, 1991), p. 5.

37   Roger Manvell, '*The Long Night* and *Le Jour se lève*', *Sight & Sound* 16/63 (Autumn 1947), p. 115.

38   Cited in Rudy Behlmer (ed.), *Memo from David O. Selznick* (New York: Modern Library, 2000), p. 217.

39   Cited in Dudley Andrew, *Mists of Regret: Culture and Sensibility in Classic French Film* (Princeton: Princeton University Press, 1995), p. 3.

40   Graham Greene, '*Hôtel du Nord*', *The Spectator* (23 June 1939), repr. in John Russell Taylor (ed.), *The Pleasure-Dome: The Collected Film Criticism of Graham Greene: 1935-1940* (London: Secker and Warburg, 1972), p. 229.

41   Gavin Lambert, 'Marcel Carné', *Sequence* (Spring 1948), p. 19.

42   Bosley Crowther, '*Daybreak*', *The New York Times* (30 July 1940), p. 27.

43   Italo Calvino, 'Autobiographie d'un spectateur', *Positif* 181 (May 1976), p. 17.

44   André Bazin, 'Jean Gabin et son destin', repr. in *Le Cinéma français de la libération à la Nouvelle Vague* (1945-1958), comp. Jean Narboni (Paris: Petite Bibliothèque des Cahiers du cinéma, 1998), p. 103.

45   In *The Whole Equation* (London: Abacus, 2004), David Thomson has noted how the differences in titles between the original film and its remake 'show how French irony seldom registers stateside', p. 283.

46   Lucy Mazdon states in *Encore Hollywood: Remaking French Cinema* (London: BFI, 2000) that there were 24 remakes of French films by American studios between 1930 and 1960.

47   Carolyn A. Durham, *Double Takes: Remaking Culture and Gender in French Films and their American Remakes* (Hanover, NH: University Press of New England, 1998), p. 11.

48   Untitled 1947 *Daily Mail* editorial, NFTVA clippings file, BFI Library, London.

49   Claude Bower, '*Le Jour se lève* "refait" et trahi', *L'Écran français*, 123 (4 November 1947), reprinted in Jacques Prévert, '*Le Jour se lève*', *L'Avant-scène cinéma* 53 (October 1965), pp. 44-5.

50   Ibid., p. 44.

51   Tom Brown, 'Les remakes de l'âge classique', in Christian Viviani (ed.), *Les Connexions françaises* (Paris: Nouveau Monde, 2007), p. 348.

52   Ibid., p. 355.

53   Ginette Vincendeau, 'Noir is also a French word: the French antecedents of film noir', in
      Ian Cameron (ed.), *The Movie Book of Film Noir* (London: Vista, 1992), p. 56.
54   James Agee, 'The Long Night', in *Agee on Film: Criticism and Comment on the Movies*
      (New York: Modern Library, 2000), p. 269.
55   Bosley Crowther, 'The Long Night', *The New York Times* (17 September 1947), p. 31.
56   Brown, 'Les remakes de l'âge classique', p. 362.
57   Susan Hayward, *French National Cinema*, 2nd edn (London: Routledge, 2005), p. 170.
58   The Métro set, built at the Joinville studios in Paris, was 120m long, 50m wide and 17m
      high. Compare this to the set for the Boulevard du Crime in *Les Enfants du paradis*,
      which was only 80m long.
59   For a comparison of *Les Portes de la nuit*'s box-office figures with other 1946 films, see
      <http://www.boxofficestars.com/1-categorie-12070757.html>. For more on *Martin
      Roumagnac* and *Les Portes de la nuit*, see Turk, *Child of Paradise*, pp. 351–8.
60   Claude Mauriac, '"Juliette" ou la clé des songes cinématographiques?', *Le Figaro littéraire*
      (26 May 1951).
61   André Bazin, 'The disincarnation of Carné', in Mary Lea Bandy (ed.), *Rediscovering
      French Film* (New York: The Museum of Modern Art, 1983), p. 131.
62   Cited in Robert Chazal, *Marcel Carné* (Paris: Seghers, 1965), p. 180. Rossellini had used
      urban-location shooting in both *Rome Open City* (1945) and *Germany Year Zero* (1947),
      and although not every location was as accurate as it claimed to be (some of the latter
      was filmed on soundstages), the depictions of Rome and Berlin were highly effective
      because they were authentic.
63   Henri Agel, *Les Grands Cinéastes* (Paris: Éditions Universitaires, 1959), p. 172.
64   Turk, *Child of Paradise*, p. 477.
65   Ibid., p. 226.
66   Ibid., pp. 173–4.
67   Ibid., p. 26.
68   Richard Dyer, 'No place for homosexuality: Marcel Carné's *L'Air de Paris* (1954)', in
      Susan Hayward and Ginette Vincendeau (eds), *French Film: Texts and Contexts*, 2nd
      edn (London and New York: Routledge, 2000), p. 127.
69   Turk, *Child of Paradise*, p. 174.
70   Ibid, p. 434
71   Bazin, 'The disincarnation of Carné', p. 131.
72   Raymond Borde and Étienne Chaumenton, *A Panorama of American Film Noir, 1941–1953*,
      trans. Paul Hammond (London: City Lights, 2000), p. 23.
73   David Mamet, 'On four favorite films', <http://www.tcm.com/this-month/article/155222|0/
      Guest-Programmer-David-Mamet.html> (accessed 24 September 2011).
74   Mark Bould, *Film Noir: From Berlin to Sin City* (London: Wallflower, 2005), p. 40.
75   The results in full were: 1. *The Bicycle Thieves* (De Sica), 2= *City Lights* (Chaplin), 2= *The
      Gold Rush* (Chaplin), 4. *Battleship Potemkin* (Eisenstein), 5= *Intolerance* (Griffith), 5=
      Louisiana Story (Flaherty), 7= *Greed* (von Stroheim), 7= *Le Jour se lève* (Carné), 7= *The
      Passion of Joan of Arc* (Dreyer), 10= *Brief Encounter* (Lean), 10= *La Règle du jeu* (Renoir).
      By the time of the next poll, in 1962, *Le Jour se lève* had dropped off the list, never to
      return. Ever since, the two more conventional 'masterpieces' of 1930s French cinema –
      L'Atalante and *La Règle du jeu* – have made at least one appearance in the Top Ten.

Conclusion

From *Le Jour se lève* I remember the angular street-corner hotel in which a suicidal Gabin is forced to hole up and the exuberantly corrupt Jules Berry and his troupe of performing dogs [...] Yes, Carné's films now impinge upon our consciousness above all as memories, memories often as potent and unshakeable as those in our own lives.[1]

Le Jour se lève, with its 'perfect inner equilibrium' and 'the happy arrangement of all [its] elements' remains Carné's most memorable film.[2] It is a pivotal work, a rich storehouse of visual and cultural themes that signals the culmination of the Poetic Realist register and, as an end product, exemplifies the structural flexibilities and visual and formal experimentation of 1930s French filmmaking practice.

Those who argue that Carné was 'simply the script's handmaiden' would do well to look at *Le Jour se lève* anew.[3] For Truffaut to declare that Carné was merely Prévert's *metteur en images* brings into clear focus the post-war French argument about the relative importance of scriptwriter and director in cinema alongside skewed assumptions about the primacy of written text over its performance. Because, in the eyes of the *Cahiers* cultural gatekeepers, Carné's entire corpus was predicated on a careful, fastidious methodology, his work would never be spoken of in the same breath as Vigo or Renoir. It is true that some of Carné's later films, like *Juliette, ou la clef des songes*, *Les Enfants du paradis* and *Les Visiteurs du soir*, can be bracketed in the *cinéma de qualité* tradition (these all possessed high production values, spectacular set pieces and a rich literary register) but these films should be placed alongside the Poetic Realist works that did much to anticipate the look and feel of French psychological *noir* of the 1950s. Such a dynamic intersecting of different styles is indicative, perhaps, not of a 'closed' director, but one open to integrating new visual and narrative approaches.

Those who criticize Carné for not 'going down the street', and denounce him for remaining in thrall to the studio aspect of filmmaking, conveniently forget that built studio sets allowed Carné to impose his vision of things onto the viewer and to compose a universe in harmony with the action. His realism always remained 'true to life' – 'fabriqué' but never 'faux' – and through stylization was nudged into the realms of the poetic. Carné never hermetically sealed out human vitality through a total subordination to design and *mise-en-scène*, but created urban spaces in which his populist narratives could unfold. But his direction could not function without Prévert's words, or Jaubert's music, or Trauner's sets, and, as such, it was a confluence of such skill and experience that enabled *Le Jour se lève* to emerge and imprint itself so fully on our consciousness. Straddling the divide between 'popular' and 'auteur', it is a film more than any other that fits the definition of classical French cinema, with its accentuated visual style, 'poetic' scripts, star actors and elegant deployment of framing, editing and camerawork. It is this 'tradition of quality' that sums up the Carné touch: professional, meticulous, harmonious. Rather than being used as a stick to beat him with, these qualities, and the blissful, woozy verbal and visual memories they conjure up, are Carné's tools of the trade, and with them, he sealed an extraordinary new cinematic style with *Le Jour se lève*: not lyrical melodrama, not film *gris*, not even Poetic Realism, but Romantic Expressionism.

Finally then, as day breaks, and Jaubert's score surges forth once more, everything that *Le Jour se lève* stands for can be summed up by this one heart-rending exchange:

FRANÇOISE: The Riviera's very beautiful, you know.

FRANÇOIS: Have you been there?

FRANÇOISE: No, but I've been told […] There are big red rocks. And then the sea, the sea with casinos all around […] It's always sunny down there […] and then the flowers […] there are mimosas all the time – even in winter.

FRANÇOIS: Mimosas! You make me laugh with your mimosas […] they're just daydreams and popular songs.

FRANÇOISE: Perhaps. But sometimes it's so dreary and sad here.

Notes

1   Gilber Adair, *Flickers: An Illustrated Celebration of 100 Years of Cinema* (London: Faber and Faber, 1995), pp. 90–1.

2   André Bazin, 'The disincarnation of Carné', in Mary Lea Bandy (ed.), *Rediscovering French Film* (New York: The Museum of Modern Art, 1983), p. 132.

3   Edward Baron Turk, *Child of Paradise: Marcel Carné and the Golden Age of French Cinema* (Cambridge, MA, and London: Harvard University Press, 1989), p. 45.

Appendix 1: Credits

Le Jour se lève
1939, France
35mm, 87 minutes
Released in Paris (Madeleine Theatre), 17 June 1939

Crew
Director: Marcel Carné
Producer: Pierre Frogerais
Production company: VOG-Sigma
Screenplay: Jacques Viot and Jacques Prévert
Additional dialogue: Jacques Prévert
Assistant directors: Pierre Blondy and Jean Fazy
Cinematography: Curt Courant (assisted by Philippe Agostini, André Bac and Albert Viguier)
Set designer: Alexandre Trauner (assisted by Paul Bertrand)
Costumes: Boris Bilinsky
Music: Maurice Jaubert
Sound: Armand Petitjean
Editor: René Le Hénaff

Cast

Jean Gabin	François
Jules Berry	Valentin
Arletty	Clara
Jacqueline Laurent	Françoise
Jacques Baumer	Chief of Police
Bernard Blier	Gaston
Mady Berry	landlady
René Génin	landlord
Marcel Pérès	Paulo
Gabrielle Fontan	old lady on staircase
Arthur Devère	Gerbois
Georges Douking	blind man
Germaine Lix	singer

Appendix 2: Marcel Carné Filmography

1929	*Nogent, eldorado du dimanche*
1936	*Jenny*
1937	*Drôle de drame*
1938	*Le Quai des brumes*
1938	*Hôtel du Nord*
1939	***Le Jour se lève***
1942	*Les Visiteurs du soir*
1945	*Les Enfants du paradis*
1946	*Les Portes de la nuit*
1950	*La Marie du port*
1954	*Juliette, ou la clef des songes*
1953	*Thérèse Raquin*
1954	*L'Air de Paris*
1956	*Le Pays d'où je viens*
1958	*Les Tricheurs*
1960	*Terrain vague*
1963	*Du mouron pour les petits oiseaux*
1965	*Trois chambres à Manhattan*
1968	*Les Jeunes Loups*
1971	*Les Assassins de l'ordre*
1974	*La Merveilleuse Visite*
1977	*La Bible*

Carné also worked as assistant director on a number of projects in the 1930s:

1928	*Les Nouveaux Messieurs* (dir. Jacques Feyder)
1929	*Cagliostro* (dir. Richard Oswald)
1930	*Sous les toits de Paris* (dir. René Clair)
1934	*Le Grand Jeu* (dir. Jacques Feyder)
1935	*Pension Mimosas* (dir. Jacques Feyder)

Appendix 3: Select Bibliography

Abel, Richard, *French Film Theory and Criticism: A History/Anthology 1907–1939*, vol. 2, *1929–1939* (Princeton: Princeton University Press, 1988).

Achard, Paul, 'Pourquoi est sifflé *Le Jour se lève*', *Ordre* (22 June 1939), n.p.

Adair, Gilbert, *Flickers: An Illustrated Celebration of 100 Years of Cinema* (London: Faber and Faber, 1995).

Affron, Charles and Mirella Jona Affron, *Sets in Motion: Art Direction and Film Narrative* (New Brunswick, NJ: Rutgers University Press, 1995).

Agee, James, 'The Long Night', in *Agee on Film: Criticism and Comment on the Movies* (New York: Modern Library, 2000), p. 269.

Agel, Henri, *Les Grands Cinéastes* (Paris: Éditions Universitaires, 1959).

Albera, François, *Albatros: Des russes à Paris 1919–1929* (Milan: Mazzotta and Cinémathèque française, 1995).

Altman, Georges, '*Le Jour se lève*: une œuvre noire et pure', *La Lumière* (16 June 1939), p. 5.

Altman, Rick, *Film/Genre* (London: BFI, 1999)

Amiel, Vincent, 'Un réalisme raisonné', *Positif* 550 (December 2006), pp. 91–2.

Andrew, Dudley, 'Poetic Realism', in Mary Lea Bandy (ed.), *Rediscovering French Film* (New York: Museum of Modern Art, 1983), pp. 115–19.

Andrew, Dudley, 'The impact of the novel on French cinema of the 30s', *L'Esprit créateur* 30:2 (1990), pp. 3–13.

Andrew, Dudley, *Mists of Regret: Culture and Sensibility in Classic French Film* (Princeton, NJ: Princeton University Press, 1995).

Andrew, Dudley and Steven Ungar, *Popular Front Paris and the Poetics of Culture* (Cambridge, MA, and London: Harvard University Press, 2005).

Anon., untitled article, *La Cinématographie française* (28 October 1938), n.p.

Anon., untitled article, *Le Petit Journal* (8 July 1938), n.p.

Anon., '*Le Jour se lève*', *Variety* (26 July 1940), p. 503.

Anon., '*Daybreak*', *Monthly Film Bulletin* 21/132 (1944), p. 47.

Aristotle, *Poetics* (London: Penguin, 1996).

Armes, Roy, *French Cinema* (London: Secker and Warburg, 1985).

Armes, Roy, 'Marcel Carné', in Christopher Lyon (ed.), *The Macmillan Dictionary of Films and Filmmakers* (London: Macmillan, 1984), vol. 2, pp. 78–9.

Arnoux, Alexandre, '*Le Jour se lève*', *Les Nouvelles littéraires* (17 June 1939), p. 10.

Bates, Robin, 'Audiences on the verge of a Fascist breakdown: male anxieties and late 1930s French Film', *Cinema Journal* 36/3 (Spring 1997), pp. 25–55.

Bazin, André, 'The Pagnol case', in Mary Lea Bandy (ed.), *Rediscovering French Film* (New York: Museum of Modern Art, 1983), pp. 92–3.

Bazin, André, 'The disincarnation of Carné', in Mary Lea Bandy (ed.), *Rediscovering French Film* (New York: The Museum of Modern Art, 1983), pp. 131–5.

Bazin, André, '*Le Jour se lève*', repr. in *Le Cinéma français de la libération à la Nouvelle Vague (1945-1958)*, comp. Jean Narboni (Paris: Petite Bibliothèque des Cahiers du cinéma, 1998), pp. 76–102.

Bazin, André, 'Jean Gabin et son destin', repr. in *Le Cinéma français de la libération à la Nouvelle Vague (1945-1958)*, comp. Jean Narboni (Paris: Petite Bibliothèque des Cahiers du cinéma, 1998), pp. 102–5.

Behlmer, Rudy (ed.), *Memo from David O. Selznick* (New York: Modern Library, 2000).

Bergfelder, Tim, Sue Harris and Sarah Street, *Film Architecture and the Transnational Imagination: Set Design in 1930s European Cinema* (Amsterdam: Amsterdam University Press, 2007).

Billard, Pierre, *L'Âge classique du cinéma français* (Paris: Flammarion, 1995).

Bizet, René, '*Le Jour se lève*', *L'Écho de Paris* (11 June 1939), n.p.

Blakeway, Claire, *Jacques Prévert: Popular French Theatre and Cinema* (London: Associated University Presses, 1990).

Borde, Raymond and Étienne Chaumenton, *A Panorama of American Film Noir, 1941-1953*, trans. Paul Hammond (London: City Lights, 2000).

Borde, Raymond, 'Dossier: la France des années 30', *L'Avant-scène cinéma* 173 (1976), pp. 23–45.

Borde, Raymond, '"The Golden Age": French cinema of the '30s', trans. Catherine A. Surowiec, in Mary Lea Bandy (ed.), *Rediscovering French Film* (New York: The Museum of Modern Art, 1983), pp. 67–81.

Bordwell, David and Kristin Thompson, *Film Art: An Introduction*, 5th edn (New York: McGraw-Hill, 1997).

Borel, Suzanne, untitled editorial, *La Cinématographie française* 1093 (14 October 1939), n.p.

Bould, Mark, *Film Noir: From Berlin to Sin City* (London: Wallflower, 2005).

Bower, Claude, '*Le Jour se lève*: "refait" et trahi', in *L'Avant-Scène cinéma* 53 (October 1965), pp. 44–5.

Bowles, Brett, 'Marcel Pagnol's *The Baker's Wife*: a cinematic charivari in Popular Front France', *The Historical Journal* 48:2 (2005), pp. 437–69.

Braudy, Leo, *The World in a Frame: What We See in Films* (New York: Anchor Press and Doubleday, 1976).

Brooke, Dinah and Nicola Hayden, Le Jour se lève: *A Film by Marcel Carné and Jacques Prévert* (New York: Simon and Schuster, 1970).

Brown, Tom, 'Les remakes de l'âge classique', in Christian Viviani (ed.), *Les Connexions françaises* (Paris: Nouveau Monde, 2007), pp. 345–75.

Burch, Noël and Geneviève Sellier, *La Drôle de guerre des sexes du cinéma français 1930-1956* (Paris: Nathan, 1996).

Burrin, Philippe, *France under the Germans: Collaboration and Compromise*, trans. Janet Lloyd (New York: New Press, 1996).

Buss, Robin, *The French through their Films* (London: Batsford, 1988).

Caine, Michael, *What's It All About?* (London: Century, 1992).

Calvino, Italo, 'Autobiographie d'un spectateur', *Positif* 181 (May 1976), pp. 13–23.

Carné, Marcel, 'La caméra, personnage du drame', *Cinémagazine* (12 July 1929), repr. in Chazal, *Marcel Carné*, pp. 87–9.

Carné, Marcel, 'Le cinéma et le monde', *Cinémagazine* (November 1932), pp. 9–12.

Carné, Marcel, 'Quand le cinéma descendra-t-il dans la rue?', *Cinémagazine* (November 1933), repr. in Robert Chazal, *Marcel Carné* (Paris: Seghers, 1965), pp. 94–6.

Carné, Marcel, *La Vie à belles dents* (Paris: Pierre Belfond, 1989).

Chapman, James, Mark Glancy and Sue Harper (eds), *The New Film History: Sources, Methods, Approaches* (Basingstoke/New York: Palgrave Macmillan, 2007).

Chazal, Robert, *Marcel Carné* (Paris: Seghers, 1965).

Chirat, Raymond, *Le Cinéma français des années trente* (Paris: Cinq Continents, 1983).

Ciment, Michel and Isabelle Jordan, 'Entretien avec Alexandre Trauner (1)', *Positif* 223 (October 1979), pp. 4–19.

Ciment, Michel, and Isabelle Jordan, 'Entretien avec Alexandre Trauner (2)', *Positif* 224 (November 1979), pp. 46–57.

Climent-Oms, Hélène, 'Carné parle', *Cahiers de la cinémathèque* 5 (Winter 1972), pp. 31–49.

Conway, Kelley, *Chanteuse in the City: The Realist Singer in French Film* (Berkeley: University of California Press, 2004).

Coquet, James de, '*Le Jour se lève*', *Le Figaro* (14 June 1939), p. 4.

Coughlan, Joseph L., '*Daybreak*', *Motion Picture Herald* (3 August 1940), p. 42.

Cousins, Mark, *The Story of Film* (London: Pavilion, 2004).

Coward, David, *The History of French Literature* (Oxford: Blackwell, 2002).

Crisp, Colin, 'The rediscovery of editing in French cinema, 1930–1945', *Histoire et mesure* 2/3 (1987), pp. 199–214.

Crisp, Colin, *The Classic French Cinema 1930–1960* (Bloomington: Indiana University Press, 1993).

Crisp, Colin, *Genre, Myth, and Convention in the French Cinema, 1929–1939* (Bloomington: Indiana University Press, 2002).

Crisp, Colin, 'Anarchy and Order in the Classic Film Industry', in Michael Temple and Michael Witt (eds), *The French Cinema Book* (London: BFI, 2004), pp. 118–27.

Crowther, Bosley, '*Daybreak*', *The New York Times* (30 July 1940), p. 27.

Crowther, Bosley, '*The Long Night*', *The New York Times* (17 September 1947), p. 31.

Dargis, Manohla, 'Ghost in the Machine', *Sight & Sound* (July 2000), pp. 20–3.

Deleuze, Gilles, *Cinema 2: The Time Image* (London: Continuum, 2005).

Douchet, Jean, and Gilles Nadeau, *Paris cinéma: Une ville vue par le cinéma de 1895 à nos jours* (Paris: Éditions du Mars, 1987).

Durgnat, Raymond, *Films and Feelings* (London: Faber and Faber, 1967).

Durgnat, Raymond 'Paint it black: the family tree of film noir', *Cinema* 6–7 (1970), pp. 49–56, repr. in Alain Silver and James Ursini (eds), *Film Noir Reader* (New York: Limelight, 1996), pp. 37–51.

Durham, Carolyn A., *Double Takes: Remaking Culture and Gender in French Films and their American Remakes* (Hanover, NH: University Press of New England, 1998).

Dyer, Richard, Stars (London: BFI, 1998).

Dyer, Richard, 'No place for homosexuality: Marcel Carné's *L'Air de Paris* (1954)', in Susan Hayward and Ginette Vincendeau (eds), *French Film: Texts and Contexts*, 2nd edn (London and New York: Routledge, 2000), pp. 127–41.

Dyer, Richard, *Heavenly Bodies* (London: Routledge, 2004).

Eder, Bruce, 'Carné and Prévert', <www.criterionco.com/asp/in_focus_essay. asp?id=9&eid=194> (accessed 1 February 2006).

Faulkner, Christopher, 'Theory and practice of film reviewing in France in the 1930s: eyes right (Lucien Rebatet and *Action française* 1936–1939)', *French Cultural Studies* 3/8 (June 1992), pp. 133–55.

Faulkner, Christopher, 'Critical debate and the construction of society', in Michael Temple and Michael Witt (eds), *The French Cinema Book* (London: BFI, 2004), pp. 172–80.

Fayard, Jean, '*Le Jour se lève*', *Candide*, 14 June 1939, p. 17.

Flitterman-Lewis, Sandy, *To Desire Differently: Feminism and the French Cinema* (Urbana and Chicago: University of Illinois Press, 1990).

Fofi, Goffredo, 'The cinema of the Popular Front (1934–1938)', *Screen* 13/4 (1972), pp. 5–57.

Forbes, Jill, *Les Enfants du paradis* (London: BFI, 1997).

Garçon, François, *De Blum à Pétain: Cinéma et société français (1936–1944)* (Paris: Éditions du Cerf, 1984).

Gauteur, Claude, *Jean Renoir: La Double Méprise 1925–1939* (Paris: Les Éditeurs français réunis, 1980).

Gauteur, Claude and Ginette Vincendeau, *Jean Gabin: Anatomie d'un mythe* (Paris: Nathan, 1993).

Greene, Graham, '*Hôtel du Nord*', *The Spectator* (23 June 1939), repr. in John Russell Taylor (ed.), *The Pleasure-Dome: The Collected Film Criticism of Graham Greene: 1935–1940* (London: Secker and Warburg, 1972), pp. 229–30.

Guillaume-Grimaud, Geneviève, *Le Cinéma du Front Populaire* (Paris: Lherminier, 1986).

Guillot, Gérard, *Les Prévert* (Paris: Seghers, 1966).

Hayward, Susan, 'Luc Besson', in Yvonne Tasker (ed.), *Fifty Contemporary Filmmakers* (London: Routledge, 2002), pp. 51–9.

Hayward, Susan, *French National Cinema*, 2nd edn (London: Routledge, 2005).

Hayward, Susan, *Cinema Studies: The Key Concepts*, 3rd edn (London and New York: Routledge, 2006).

Hedges, Inez, 'Form and meaning in the French film, I: time and space', *The French Review* 14/1 (1980), pp. 28–36.

Hoffmann, Stanley, *La Société bloquée* (Paris: Le Seuil, 1970).

Jackson, Julien, *The Popular Front in France* (Cambridge: Cambridge University Press, 1988)

Jaubert, Maurice, 'Music on the screen', in Charles Davy (ed.), *Footnotes to the Film* (London: Lovat Dickson Ltd, 1938), pp. 101–15.

Jeancolas, Jean-Pierre, 'Cinéma des années trente: la crise et l'image de la crise', *Le Mouvement social* 154 (January–March 1991), pp. 173–95.

Jeancolas, Jean-Pierre, *Le Cinéma des français: 15 ans d'années trente (1929–1944)* (Paris: Nouveau monde, 2005).

Jeancolas, Jean-Pierre, 'Cinéma et réalisme III: France 1895–1950', *Les Cahiers du 7e Art* 8 (1989), pp. 1–56.

Jeancolas, Jean-Pierre, 'Beneath the despair, the show goes on: Marcel Carné's *Les Enfants du paradis* (1943–5)', trans. by Marianne Johnson, in Susan Hayward and Ginette Vincendeau (eds), *French Film: Texts and Contexts*, 2nd edn (London and New York: Routledge, 2000), pp. 78–88.

Kael, Pauline, *5001 Nights at the Movies* (New York and London: Marion Boyars, 1993).

Kael, Pauline, *Raising Kane and Other Essays* (New York and London: Marion Boyars, 1996).

Kemp, Philip, '*Le Jour se lève*', <http://www.filmreference.com/Films-Im-Le/Le-Jour-se-L-ve.html> (accessed 1 March 2009).

Kennedy, Maev, 'Soul of Paris – iconic images go on show', *Guardian* (22 February 2001), p. 5.

Kracauer, Siegfried, *From Caligari to Hitler: A Psychological Study of the German Film* (Princeton, NJ: Princeton University Press, 1947).

Lagny, Michèle, Marie-Claire Ropars and Pierre Sorlin, *Générique des années 30* (Vincennes: Presses Universitaires de Vincennes, 1986).

Lanzoni, Rémi Fournier, *French Cinema: From its Beginnings to the Present* (New York: Continuum, 2004).

Larkin, Maurice, *France Since the Popular Front: Government and People 1936–1986* (New York: Oxford University Press, 1988).

Mac Orlan, Pierre, *Masques sur mesure* (Paris: Gallimard, 1965).

Mamet, David, 'On four favorite films', <http://www.tcm.com/this-month/article/155222|0/Guest-Programmer-David-Mamet.html> (accessed 24 September 2011).

Manvell, Roger, '*The Long Night* and *Le Jour se lève*', *Sight & Sound* 16/63 (Autumn 1947), pp. 115–16.

Mauriac, Claude, '"Juliette" ou la clé des songes cinématographiques?', *Le Figaro littéraire* (26 May 1951).

Mazdon, Lucy, *Encore Hollywood: Remaking French Cinema* (London: BFI, 2000).

Mezzanine, '*Le Jour se lève*', *Marianne* (21 June 1939), p. 19.

Mitry, Jean, 'Réalisme poétique', in Jean Mitry, *Histoire du cinéma: Art et industrie*, vol. 4, *1930–1940* (Paris: Jean-Pierre Delarge, 1980), pp. 325–54.

Naremore, James, *More Than Night: Film Noir in its Contexts* (Berkeley: University of California Press, 2008).

O'Brien, Charles, 'Film noir in France: before the liberation', *Iris* 21 (Spring 1996), pp. 7–20.

Orpen, Valerie, *Film Editing: The Art of the Expressive* (London: Wallflower, 2003)

Perez, Michel, *Les Films de Carné* (Paris: Ramsay, 1986).

Phillips, Alastair, 'The camera goes down the streets: *Dans les rues* (Victor Trivas, 1933) and the Paris of the German émigrés', *Modern and Contemporary France* 8/3 (2000), pp. 325–34.

Phillips, Alastair, 'Migration and exile in the classical period', in Michael Temple and Michael Witt (eds), *The French Cinema Book* (London: BFI, 2004), pp. 103–17.

Place, Janey, 'Women in film noir', in E. Ann Kaplan (ed.), *Women in Film Noir* (BFI: London, 1997), pp. 47–68.

Porcile, François, '*Le Jour se lève*: une partition de Maurice Jaubert', <http://www. forumdesimages.net/fr/alacarte/htm/ETUDE/LEJOURSELÈVE /content.htm> (accessed 8 November 2006).

Powell, Dilys, 'Since 1939', repr. in Christopher Cook (ed.), *The Dilys Powell Film Reader* (Manchester: Carcanet, 1991).

Powell, Dilys, 'Film directors – a talk for the BBC's Third Programme, October 1946', repr. in Christopher Cook (ed.), *The Dilys Powell Film Reader* (Manchester: Carcanet, 1991).

Prédal, René, *La société française 1914–1945 à travers le cinéma* (Paris: Armand Colin, 1972).

Prévert, Jacques, '*Le Jour se lève*', *L'Avant-scène cinéma* 53 (October 1965), pp. 7–40.

Prévert, Jacques, *Anthologie Prévert*, ed. Christiane Mortelier (London: Routledge, 1981).

Reader, Keith, '"Mon cul est intersexuel?": Arletty's performance of gender', in Alex Hughes and James S. Williams (eds), *Gender and French Cinema* (Berg: Oxford/ New York, 2001).

Rebatet [i.e. François Vinneuil], '*Jenny*', *Action française*, <http://www.marcel-Carné. com/filmographie/jenny.html#revue> (accessed 1 March 2009).

Rebatet, 'L'écran de la semaine: *La Bête humaine*', *Action française*, 30 December 1938, n.p.

Rotha, Paul, *The Film till Now: A Survey of World Cinema* (London: Vision Press, 1949).

Roud, Richard, 'Jean Renoir: to 1939', *Cinema: A Critical Dictionary* (London: Secker and Warburg, 1980), vol. 2, pp. 835–45.

Sadoul, Georges, *Histoire du cinéma mondial des origines à nos jours* (Paris: Flammarion, 1949).

Sadoul, Georges, 'À propos de quelques films récents', in *Écrits 1: Chroniques de cinéma français 1939–1967* (Paris: Union Générale d'Éditions, 1978), pp. 11–17.

Sautet, Claude, '*Le Jour se lève*', *Positif* (June 1994), p. 126.

Schrader, Paul, 'Notes on film noir', *Film Comment* 8/1 (Spring 1972), pp. 8–13.

Siclier, Jacques, *La Femme fatale dans le cinéma français* (Paris: Éditions du Cerf, 1957).

Strebel, Elizabeth Grottle, 'French social cinema and the Popular Front', *Journal of Contemporary History* 12/3 (July 1977), pp. 499–519.

Surowiec, Catherine A., 'Maurice Jaubert: poet of music', in Mary Lea Bandy (ed.), *Rediscovering French Film* (New York: The Museum of Modern Art, 1983), pp. 87–8.

Temple, Michael and Michael Witt, 'Introduction 1930–60: classicism and conflict', in Michael Temple and Michael Witt (eds), *The French Cinema Book* (London: BFI, 2004), pp. 93–102.

Thiher, Allen, *The Cinematic Muse: Critical Studies in the History of French Cinema* (Columbia and London: University of Missouri Press, 1979).

Thomson, David, 'The art of the art director', *American Film* 2/4 (1977), pp. 12–20.

Thomson, David, *The New Biographical Dictionary of Film* (London: Little, Brown, 2003).

Thomson, David, *The Whole Equation: A History of Hollywood* (London: Abacus, 2004).

Truffaut, François, '*Le Pays d'où je viens*', *Arts; lettres; spectacles*, 31 October–6 November 1956.

Turim, Maureen, *Flashbacks in Film: Memory and History* (New York: Routledge, 1989).

Turim, Maureen, 'The displacement of architecture in avant-garde films', *Iris* 12 (1991), pp. 25–38.

Turim, Maureen, 'Poetic idealism as psychoanalytical and ideological operation: Marcel Carné's *Le Jour se lève* (1939)', in Susan Hayward and Ginette Vincendeau (eds), *French Film: Texts and Contexts*, 2nd edn (London: Routledge, 2000), pp. 63–77.

Turk, Edward Baron, *Child of Paradise: Marcel Carné and the Golden Age of French Cinema* (Cambridge, MA, and London: Harvard University Press, 1989).

Vanoosthuyse, François, '*Le Jour se lève*, identification d'un prolétaire', *CinémAction* 98 (2001), pp. 66–72.

Villelaur, Anne, '*Le Jour se lève*', *Dossiers du cinéma, Collection Rondel* 4* SW 8271 (Paris: Bibliothèque de l'Arsenal), p. 117.

Vincendeau, Ginette, 'Community, nostalgia and the spectacle of masculinity', *Screen* 26/6 (1985), pp. 18–38.

Vincendeau, Ginette, 'Daddy's girl: oedipal narratives in 1930s French films', *Iris* 5/1 (1988), pp. 70–81.

Vincendeau, Ginette, 'From the *bal populaire* to the casino: class and leisure in French films of the 1930s', *Nottingham French Studies* 31/2 (1992), pp. 52–70.

Vincendeau, Ginette, 'Noir is also a French word: the French antecedents of film noir', in Ian Cameron (ed.), *The Movie Book of Film Noir* (London: Vista, 1992), pp. 49–58.

Vincendeau, Ginette, 'Anatomy of a myth: Jean Gabin', *Nottingham French Studies* 32/1 (Spring 1993), pp. 19–31.

Vincendeau, Ginette, *Pépé le Moko* (London: BFI, 1998).

Vincendeau, Ginette, *Stars and Stardom in French Cinema* (London and New York: Continuum, 2000).

Vincendeau, Ginette, 'The art of spectacle: the aesthetics of classical French cinema', in Michael Temple and Michael Witt (eds), *The French Cinema Book* (London: BFI, 2004), pp. 137–52.

Vuillermoz, Émile, '*Le Jour se lève*', *Le Temps* (17 June 1939), p. 5.

Williams, Alan, *Republic of Images: A History of French Filmmaking* (Cambridge, MA, and London: Harvard University Press, 1992).

Winnington, Richard, *Drawn and Quartered* (London: Saturn, 1948).

Wood, Gaby, 'Seeing in the dark', *Guardian Weekend* (15 July 2000), pp. 10–16.

Index